高校英语选修课系列教材

U0365807

英语品中国
科技篇

主 编 张钫炜
副主编 赵 欣 袁 方 王姗姗
编 者 郝劲梅 李 俊 沈炳坤

清华大学出版社
北 京

内 容 简 介

　　本教材精选语言地道、立场正确、紧跟时代的英语文章，向学生展示中国科技故事的多彩画卷。教材紧扣时事热点，围绕科技创新驱动民族伟大复兴，探讨 5G 发展、中国创造、电子支付、在线教育、中医科学、建筑设计、知识共享、社交媒体等话题，在呈现中国科技盛宴的同时，突出科技背后的中国精神。本教材依托产出导向法，围绕交际场景完成产出驱动、输入促成和产出评价的教学流程，落实"学用一体"的理念。同时，在全人教育理念的引领下，本教材引导学生在学习语言的同时，提升爱国情怀和个人综合素养。教材有配套慕课"中国文化传承与科技创新"，在中国大学慕课网开放，还有电子版教师用书和 PPT 课件，读者可登录 www.tsinghuaelt.com 下载使用。

　　本教材适用于大学本科学生的选修课，也适合研究生作为公共英语课程教材，同时还适合对中国科技故事感兴趣的读者作为课外阅读材料。

图书在版编目（CIP）数据

英语品中国：科技篇 / 张钫炜主编 . —北京：清华大学出版社，2021.11（2025.3 重印）
高校英语选修课系列教材
ISBN 978-7-302-59323-2

Ⅰ. ①英…　Ⅱ. ①张…　Ⅲ. ①英语—高等学校—教材　Ⅳ. ① H319.39

中国版本图书馆 CIP 数据核字（2021）第 205504 号

责任编辑：刘　艳
封面设计：子　一
责任校对：王凤芝
责任印制：宋　林

出版发行：清华大学出版社
　　　　网　　址：https://www.tup.com.cn, https://www.wqxuetang.com
　　　　地　　址：北京清华大学学研大厦 A 座　邮　编：100084
　　　　社 总 机：010-83470000　　　　　　邮　购：010-62786544
　　　　投稿与读者服务：010-62776969, c-service@tup.tsinghua.edu.cn
　　　　质量反馈：010-62772015, zhiliang@tup.tsinghua.edu.cn
印 装 者：涿州市般润文化传播有限公司
经　　销：全国新华书店
开　　本：185mm×260mm　　印　张：13　　字　数：253 千字
版　　次：2021 年 11 月第 1 版　　　　　印　次：2025 年 3 月第 3 次印刷
定　　价：58.00 元

产品编号：091254-02

前 言

2016 年，习近平总书记在全国高校思想政治工作会议上指出："要坚持把立德树人作为中心环节，把思想工作贯穿教育教学全过程，实现全程育人、全方位育人，努力开创我国高等教育事业发展新局面。"2020 年，教育部印发《高等学校课程思政建设指导纲要》，全面推进高校课程思政建设。同时，国家高度重视讲好中国故事，传播好中国声音，展示真实、立体、全面的中国。外语课程有其天然的文明交流互鉴的土壤，教师应该引导每一位学生参与到讲好中国故事的实践中来，结合专业特色，展示丰富多彩、生动立体的中国形象，提升学生的文化自信和家国情怀，同时也提高他们的思辨能力。

从 2015 年开始，编者团队在北京邮电大学搭建了讲好中国故事的生态体系，开设了面向不同学习对象（中国学生和外国学生）、使用不同教学范式（线上、线下）和模态（音频、视频、文本、图片等）的系列课程，设计了大量讲中国故事的情境，寓价值引领于知识传授。在多年的教学实践中，编者团队发现讲好中国故事教学领域教材建设的不足，对当下中国故事，尤其是科技故事的关注更不足，教学设计也不够系统。为此，编写团队将思政理念贯穿于教学实践的各个环节，打造学思践悟的教学闭环，经过反复设计打磨，尝试在"新工科"和"新文科"建设的大背景下，将科技与文化内容交叉融合，拓宽学生的国际视野，塑造学生爱国、理性、自信的价值观，推动中国本土文化主导的话语体系建设。

本教材主要有以下几个特点：

1. 内容上关注中国科技故事的多渠道与多领域

本教材选取了近两年英语世界知名媒体对中国科技文化领域所做的报道和评论文章，如美国的《纽约时报》（*The New York Times*）和英国的《卫报》（*The Guardian*），所选话题均为当下热点，议题涉及互联网科技、在线教育、社交媒体等，能够帮助当代大学生更好地了解英语世界的写作者如何认识和解读中国，学习地道的写作语言与风格，批判吸收不同文化下的价值探讨。

2. 设计上采用产出导向教学法

本教材的编写依托产出导向教学法，同时适用于混合式教学模式。每个单元学习由"驱动—促成—评价"三个环节组成。在单元学习伊始的"驱动"环节，学生通过观看相应的慕课内容积累与主题相关的基础知识，并思考、尝试完成 Pretest 模块中的基础知识小测验和 Pretask 模块中的情境语言任务，以检验该阶段的学习效果，促使学生产生完成任务的意愿，也帮助他们了解自己的不足。在"促成"环节，经过教师讲解，学生可对文章进行精读或泛读，从而对单元主题有进一步的认识和思考，完成循序渐进的练习：Prepare/Probe 模块主要解决文章理解、结构分析等基础问题；Practice 模块对于词汇、句式和语篇给出了不同的针对性练习；Produce 模块是综合应用模块。学生经过前期的学习，已经掌握了完成任务的语言文化知识，因此在该环节主要进行单元任务相关的技能学习，通过分步骤、分阶段的子任务逐步完成单元任务，最终通过教师评价，完成单元最后的量表，以实现师生共评的"评价"环节。各学习阶段设置清晰，有助于教师选择性地安排学习内容，也有利于学生自学。上述流程具体如下图所示：

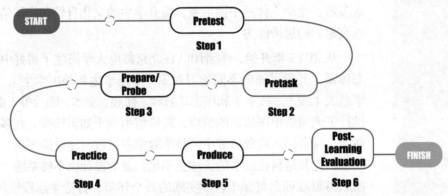

3. 独创知识目标、技能目标、价值目标三位一体的清单

在每一章最后，编者团队都从知识、技能、价值三个维度来考量学生的掌握情况，将思政目标指标化，也能帮助广大教师落实课程思政的教学效果。这样的教学尝试也得到了专家的认可和肯定。编者团队基于此设计的课程思政教学范式获得了外语教学课程思政大赛全国二等奖和教育部课程思政教学示范课程称号，授课团队入选国家级课程思政教学名师和教学团队。

另外，课程团队持续建设慕课"中国文化传承与科技创新"，同时在北京高等教育本科教学改革创新项目和教育部课程思政教学示范项目的支持下，构建四维协同、拼图式、嵌入型、智能化英语讲好中国故事全域资源库，后续也会通过清华大学出版社线上资源平台分享给选用本教材的教师，以帮助其进行个性化的教学设计。

本教材文章长度在 1 200~1 800 词之间，生词选取标准为大学英语四级（不含）以上单词，文章后所列的术语表还有助于学生对相关科技英语词汇的积累。教材还充分考虑到工科院校学生用英语讲好中国故事的场景和情境，在产出任务上设计了概要撰写、会议通知撰写、海报设计等具体任务。本教材可以作为本科阶段高阶学生选修课和研究生阶段公共英语课程的教材。

对于本教材的编写，中国科学院大学的彭工教授提出了诸多宝贵意见，北京邮电大学的夏增艳副教授、武永副研究员和许可老师进行了配套课件的制作，在此一并表示感谢。

编者

2021 年 6 月

Contents

Chapter 1

China's Communication Technology

Pretest

How much do you know about the development of the Internet and its application in China? Can you tell whether the following statements are true or false? You can go to our MOOC (5.1 Life in the Digital Age—Introduction; 5.4 Life in the Digital Age—Smart City) to learn more before taking this quiz. Write T for true and F for false.

1) From 1994 when China was first connected to the Internet, the information flow was via one-way spreading through the portal search sites. (   )

2) Internet plus, paid knowledge, we-media and sharing economy are the results of the second Internet wave in China. (   )

3) The first person who brought the core Internet technology from the U.S. to China was Jack Ma, the chief engineer of China's Internet industry. (   )

4) BAT refers to Baidu, Airbnb and Tencent. (   )

5) Baidu is one of the largest search engines in the world. (   )

6) The name Baidu was inspired by a famous line from a Chinese poem: "Hundreds of thousands of times, for her I searched in chaos." (   )

7) Smart city features infrastructure interlinked by software, hardware, management, computing, data analysis and other services. (   )

8) Huawei engaged in the construction of smart city programs in other countries. (   )

9) IoT technology has not yet been applied to the building of smart cities. (   )

10) Hangzhou collaborated with Ericsson and ZTE to build the "City Brain" project. (   )

Pretask

You are currently working as an intern in the 5G department of Huawei, and you have been asked to write an essay to explain the similarities and differences between 4G and 5G to ordinary Internet users. You have found an online article on 5G, and your colleague advises you to read through it to get ideas.

1) To accomplish the task, I plan to take the following steps:

_____.

For the first step, I think _____

might be challenging.

For the second step, I think _____

might be challenging.

_____

_____

2) I expect to achieve the following goals after learning the unit:

_____

_____

Passage
When Is 5G Coming to China?

This article is adapted from Tim Fisher[1]'s article from Lifewire[2] (January, 2021). The author presents the current development of 5G in China, analyzes the advantages of 5G over 4G, introduces 5G rollout plans of various Chinese companies, lists the challenges to the faster rollout of 5G, and looks into the prospects of 6G. Mark his words "5G uses different kinds of antennas, operates on different radio spectrum frequencies, connects many more devices to the Internet, minimizes delays, and delivers ultrafast speeds".

make sense
to be reasonable or logical or comprehensible

1   Parts of China have 5G access right now, and lots more are coming. The country already leads the world in the mobile market sector, so it **makes sense** that it'll reach the top in terms of 5G users. GSMA[3] estimates 460 million 5G connections in China by 2025.

2   In other words, 5G in China will be a much bigger thing than 5G...well, anywhere.

3   Currently, there are a few primary next-gen players

---

1 Tim Fisher is the General Manager and VP of Lifewire.com. He has over 20 years' experience in writing in the technology space and his expertise is in troubleshooting & support, smart home technology, Android & iOS, technology concepts, 5G & wireless networks and Internet research.
2 Lifewire is a top ten technology information website, as rated by comScore, a leading Internet measurement company. It reaches more than 10 million readers per month with answers to their most pressing technology questions.
3 The GSMA (Global System for Mobile Communications Association) represents the interests of mobile operators worldwide, uniting nearly 800 operators with almost 300 companies in the broader mobile ecosystem.

that are bringing about this **ultrafast** new wireless technology. It's only a matter of time before you can take advantage of all that 5G will offer in your area.

5G Wireless Technology

4   5G is the next generation of mobile networking technology following 4G. Much like every generation before it, 5G aims to make mobile communication faster and more reliable as more and more devices go online.

5   Unlike in the past, when mobile networks only needed to support cell phones that were just for browsing the web and text messaging, we now have all sorts of bandwidth[4]-demanding devices like our HD-streaming smartphones, smartwatches with data plans, always-on security cameras, self-driving and Internet-connected cars, and other **promising** devices like health sensors and **untethered** AR and VR hardware.

6   As billions more devices connect to the web, the entire **infrastructure** needs to **accommodate** the traffic to not only support faster connections but also better handle **simultaneous** ones and provide broader coverage for these devices. This is what 5G is all about.

Benefits of 5G over 4G

7   If you're not familiar, this is the next generation of wireless technology. When comparing 5G with 4G, we see faster speeds and much lower **delays**, which for you, means accessing data more quickly and having a smoother experience when watching movies, playing games, browsing the web, etc.

ultrafast /'ʌltrəˌfɑːst/ *adj.* extremely fast

promising /'prɒmɪsɪŋ/ *adj.* showing signs of being good or successful

untethered /ʌn'teðəd/ *adj.* not tied or limited with or as if with a tether

infrastructure /'ɪnfrəstrʌktʃə(r)/ *n.* the basic systems and services that are necessary for a country or an organization to run smoothly, for example, buildings, transport, and water and power supplies

accommodate /ə'kɒmədeɪt/ *v.* to provide enough space for sb./sth.

simultaneous /ˌsɪml'teɪnɪəs/ *adj.* happening or done at the same time as sth. else

delay /dɪ'leɪ/ *n.* a period of time when sb./sth. has to wait because of a problem that makes sth. slow or late

---

4 Bandwidth refers to the amount of data that can be moved (uploaded or downloaded) through a network over a given time.

8 5G is simply the next numbered generation following 4G, which replaced all the older technologies.

- 1G introduced analog voice;
- 2G introduced digital voice;
- 3G ushered in mobile data;
- 4G paved the way for widespread mobile Internet usage.

9 5G is the newest mobile network that's replacing the current 4G technology by providing a number of improvements in speed, coverage, and **reliability**. The primary focus and reason for needing an **upgraded** network are to support the growing number of devices that demand Internet access, many of them requiring so much bandwidth in order to function normally that 4G simply doesn't cut it anymore.

10 5G uses different kinds of antennas, operates on different radio spectrum frequencies, connects many more devices to the Internet, minimizes delays, and **delivers** ultrafast speeds.

China's 5G Rollout Plans

11 Three wireless carriers launched their new networks on October 31, 2019: China Mobile, China Unicom, and China Telecom. A few others have a network up and running now as well, or are looking into a 5G launch in China this year.

12 However, none of these companies currently provide **widespread** 5G coverage until January 2021. The largest cities that have 5G access in China include Beijing, Shanghai, and Shenzhen.

---

reliability
/rɪˌlaɪəˈbɪləti/
n. the quality or state of being reliable

upgrade /ˈʌpˌɡreɪd/
v. to improve sth. (especially machinery) by raising it to a higher grade (as by adding or replacing components)

deliver /dɪˈlɪvə(r)/
v. to produce or provide what people expect you to

widespread
/ˈwaɪdspred/
adj. existing or happening over a large area or among many people

China Mobile 5G

13   China Mobile has made 5G **available** in Beijing, Shanghai, and nearly 50 other cities. Being the world's biggest mobile phone operator with nearly one billion **subscribers**, there's no doubt that they'**re on track** to deliver its customers a new, faster network.

14   The 5G plan from China Mobile is available for less than $20 and gets you 30 GB of data at a max speed of 300 Mbps.

15   China Mobile researched 5G technology with Ericsson[5] in 2015, set up a 5G base station in June of 2017 in Guangdong, and launched another 5G trial network in Beijing just a month later. It even has a 5G network in the Hongqiao Railway Station.

16   Huawei, a Chinese technology giant, has collaborated with China Mobile through strategic collaboration. In 2019, Huawei won most of 5G network equipment contracts in a recent **procurement** from China Mobile.

China Unicom 5G

17   China Unicom is the world's fourth largest mobile service provider. With such a large subscriber base, it makes sense that it's one of the front runners of 5G in China.

18   Before China Unicom's 5G launch, it had a fifth-gen network set up in very few locations since most, if not all of them, were test projects, with the exception of a few.

19   Some of the 5G cities mentioned by them include Beijing, Tianjin, Qingdao, Hangzhou, Nanjing,

---

5 Ericsson is a Swedish multinational networking and telecommunications company headquartered in Stockholm.

available /ə'veɪləbl/
adj. (of things) that you can get, buy or find

subscriber /səb'skraɪbə(r)/
n. a person who pays to receive a service

on track
to achieve or do what is necessary or expected

procurement /prə'kjʊəmənt/
n. the process of obtaining supplies of sth., especially for a government or an organization

Wuhan, Guiyang, Chengdu, Fuzhou, Zhengzhou, and Shenyang. The plan is that each of these locations will build 100 5G base stations.

20   At the end of 2020, China Unicom and Huawei jointly announced the achievements of the "5G Capital" innovation project with the theme of "Smarter, Together". The "5G Capital" innovation project is part of the two companies' broader efforts to build Beijing into a global **benchmark** for 5G applications.

China Telecom 5G

21   China Telecom has launched 5G in a subway station in Chengdu called Taipingyuan Station. There's also coverage in airports and other areas of Hubei.

22   In August 2020, Huawei and China Telecom Shenzhen jointly launched a pilot site that binds 5G Super Uplink and downlink carrier aggregation (CA). This pilot innovatively **leverages** Super Uplink to maximize uplink coverage and experience, as well as fully utilizes downlink CA to deliver optimal user experience.

5G Challenges: Why It Isn't Rolling Out Faster

5G Network Deployment Challenges

23   Due to the type of signal that 5G cell towers **transmit**, their reach is severely limited to devices in close **proximity**. Many networks are operating on 5G radio frequencies called millimeter waves that are capable of carrying lots of data. So, while 5G networks support faster connections and streaming, they are often limited to less than one square mile of coverage.

---

benchmark
/'bentʃmɑːk/
n. sth. that can be measured and used as a standard that other things can be compared with

leverage /'liːvərɪdʒ/
v. to use or to exploit

transmit /trænz'mɪt/
v. to send an electronic signal, radio or television broadcast, etc.
proximity /prɒk'sɪməti/
n. the state of being near sb./sth. in distance or time

---

24 Because of 5G's limited scope, fewer users can access 5G from a single cell tower. 5G signals are also more easily blocked by common objects like trees and buildings. This means that many small antennas have to be **erected** to serve more customers. Deploying such infrastructure across the nation isn't an easy task, and providers are running into issues with local community regulations.

erect /ɪˈrekt/
v. to put sth. in position and make it stand vertical

Testing Is Crucial

25 Like all developing technologies, **rigorous** testing must be completed before an actual 5G **rollout** can take place. Companies won't **release** a new product or service until they're confident that it will work as advertised and provide the best experience for the customer. Most major mobile phone operators around the world have been testing 5G indoors and outdoors for a while now. Some companies are testing 5G in moving vehicles and others via fixed wireless access points.

rigorous /ˈrɪɡərəs/
adj. done carefully and with a lot of attention to detail
rollout /ˈrəʊl aʊt/
n. the widespread public introduction of a new product
release /rɪˈliːs/
v. to make sth. available to the public

5G Phones Aren't Yet Mainstream

26 Some phone carriers have yet to release 5G phones, and many consumers don't feel the need to buy them yet since they're unusable where they live or travel. Other people are also concerned about how safe 5G radio waves are given that it's a new type of network that operates at different radio frequencies than older networks like 4G and 3G.

5G Rollout Is Expensive

27 The deployment of a brand-new mobile network isn't cheap. Telecom companies are expected to invest as much as $275 billion into 5G infrastructure before 2025. A mobile network operator has to pay for all of the following (and more) during a 5G rollout before it can even reach customers:

- Spectrum licensing;
- The physical hardware used in the 5G deployment;
- Hiring technicians to install the necessary hardware;
- Testing and retesting of the network;
- Deployment fees demanded by regulators.

6G in China

28　With 5G networks still being deployed around the world and many areas of the globe still using 4G and even 3G networks, it seems a bit early to throw around the term 6G. After all, what use do we have for 6G networks when relatively few people can even use a 5G network?

29　That said, technology always pushes forward and standards take a long time to mature, so we've always been on a path to a 6G world. If anything, the idea of 6G this early in the development of 5G simply **indicates** how quickly this technology moves forward. We've managed to go from 1G to 5G in such a relatively short amount of time, so 6G is just the natural **progression** towards faster and better wireless connectivity.

30　In China there are some **clues** that 6G development is already in its early stages. Not long after 5G came to China was it clear that 6G would start being worked on. Research institutes, universities, and government departments are already researching 6G before most of the world has had a taste for 5G. In late 2020 China sent a 6G satellite into **orbit** to test ultra-high speeds using terahertz waves.

31　China's Ministry of Industry and Information Technology, which first started their 6G research in March of 2018, claims that a commercial version of

indicate /ˈɪndɪkeɪt/
v. to show that sth. is true or exists

progression /prəˈgreʃn/
n. the process of developing gradually from one stage or state to another

clue /kluː/
n. a fact or a piece of evidence that helps you discover the answer to a problem

orbit /ˈɔːbɪt/
n. a curved path followed by a planet or an object as it moves around another planet, star, moon, etc.

the sixth generation of wireless technology will be released by 2030.

(1,511 words)

Theme-Related Words & Expressions

5G access	5G 接入
GSMA	全球移动通信系统协会
5G connection	5G 连接
next-gen player	下一代玩家
mobile networking technology	移动网络技术
HD-streaming smartphone	高清直播智能手机
Internet-connected car	联网汽车
health sensor	健康传感器
AR hardware	增强现实硬件
VR hardware	虚拟现实硬件
traffic	流量
analog voice	模拟语音
Internet access	互联网接入
radio spectrum frequency	无线电频谱频率
China Mobile	中国移动
China Unicom	中国联通
China Telecom	中国电信
downlink carrier aggregation	下行载波聚合
uplink coverage	上行覆盖范围
5G coverage	5G 覆盖
Ericsson	爱立信公司
base station	基站
millimeter wave	毫米波
cell tower	发射塔
antenna	天线
fixed wireless access point	固定无线接入点
spectrum licensing	频谱许可
wireless connectivity	无线连接
terahertz wave	太赫兹波

China's Ministry of Industry and Information Technology	中国工信部
Digital China	数字中国
Optical Network	光网
Connectivity	互联互通
Data Silos	数据孤岛
Internet Power	网络强国
East Data, West Computing	东数西算
Computing Power Network	算力网络
Quantum Information	量子信息
Blockchain	区块链
Cloud Computing	云计算

Prepare/Probe

❶ Reading Comprehension

Answer the following questions according to the passage.

1) What effects will 5G exert on mobile communication?

2) What are the advantages of 5G over 4G?

3) Which Chinese companies started their 5G networks in October, 2019? Which one currently provides widespread 5G coverage?

4) Since 5G has not been widely covered, why do we talk about the rollout of 6G networks?

5) What are the clues that indicate 6G technology is already in its initial phase in China?

_____

_____

⑪ Structure Building

Check your understanding of the overall structure of the passage by completing the following diagram.

Overview of 5G in China	
China's 5G enjoys a promising prospect. (Paras. 1–3)	• It can be expected that China will reach the top in terms of 1) _____ . • It's only a matter of 2) _____ before you can take advantage of all that 5G will offer in your area.
5G Wireless Technology	
5G is the next generation of mobile networking technology following 4G. (Paras. 4–6)	• In the past: Mobile networks only needed to support cell phones that were just for browsing the web and text messaging. • Now: Various 3) _____ devices are available.
Benefits of 5G over 4G	
5G has many advantages over 4G. (Paras. 7–10)	• Faster speeds; • Lower 4) _____ ; • Improved coverage and 5) _____ .
China's 5G Rollout Plans	
Several companies have a 5G network up and running and they have all collaborated with Huawei to launch 5G projects. (Paras. 11–22)	• China Mobile: The 5G plan is available for less than $20 and gets you 30 GB of data at a max speed of 300 Mbps. • China Unicom: In each of the 5G cities mentioned by them, 6) _____ 5G base stations will be built. • China Telecom: 5G coverage is available in a subway station of Chengdu and in airports and other areas of Hubei.

Continued

5G Challenges: Why It Isn't Rolling Out Faster	
Due to the type of signal that 5G cell towers transmit, their reach is severely limited to devices in close proximity. (Paras. 23–27)	• Testing: Rigorous testing must be completed before an actual 5G rollout can take place. • 5G phones aren't yet 7) _____. • The deployment of a brand-new mobile network is 8) _____.
6G in China	
There are some clues that 6G development is already in its early stages in China. (Paras. 28–31)	• In late 2020: China sent a 6G satellite into orbit to test 9) _____ speeds. • By 2030: A(n) 10) _____ version of 6G is expected to be released.

Practice

❶ Vocabulary Practice

1. **Match the following theme-related words and expressions in Column A with their Chinese equivalents in Column B.**

Column A	Column B
1) wireless connectivity	A. 5G 蜂窝基站
2) HD-streaming smartphone	B. 中国移动
3) health sensor	C. 增强现实硬件
4) AR hardware	D. 无线连接
5) Internet-connected car	E. 基站
6) VR hardware	F. 发射塔
7) 5G cell site	G. 中国联通
8) base station	H. 中国电信
9) GSMA	I. 高清直播智能手机
10) cell tower	J. 虚拟现实硬件
11) China Mobile	K. 全球移动通信系统协会

12) China Unicom   L. 联网汽车

13) China Telecom   M. 中国工信部

14) China's Ministry of Industry   N. 健康传感器

    and Information Technology

2. **Group the words and expressions related to 5G in Exercise 1. Start with the examples given below.**

5G operators	*China Mobile;* _____
5G regulators	*GSMA;* _____
5G infrastructure	*5G cell site;* _____
Bandwidth-demanding devices	*HD-streaming smartphone;* _____

3. **Fill in the blanks with the words in the box. Change the form if necessary.**

> leverage   clue   delay   infrastructure   benchmark
> simultaneous   subscriber   indicate   orbit   ultra-fast

1) The State Council called for new _____ development, including 5G, artificial intelligence, industrial Internet and some other areas to offset the economic impact of the pandemic and boost sustainable growth.

2) You've accessed an article available only to _____.

3) Most satellites function for years after entering the _____, but eventually, they have to end their missions and burn up into the atmosphere due to fuel exhaustion.

4) Our company provides _____ interpretation equipment, including soundproof cabins, headsets (15 channels), microphones, and the transmission equipment.

5) The material could be used to make _____ transistors because electrons move through it at extremely high speeds.

6) We can gain a market advantage by _____ our network of partners.

7) Tests at the age of seven provide a(n) _____ against which the child's progress at school can be measured.

8) Record profits in the retail market _____ a boom in the economy.

9) In China there are some _____ that 6G development is already in its early stages.

10) This airline company understands the inconvenience of flight _____ and will try its best to minimize the impact of these disruptions.

Ⅱ Sentence Practice

Study the sentence structure first, and then translate each of the given Chinese sentences into English by imitating the sentence structure.

For example:

At the same time, however, such problems as greenhouse gas emissions and ozone depletion have become more evident in the field of environment.

翻译：但是，与此同时，互联网领域发展不平衡、规则不健全、秩序不合理等问题日益凸显。

At the same time, however, such problems as imbalanced development, inadequate rules and inequitable order have become more evident in the field of the Internet.

1) The country already leads the world in the mobile market sector, so it makes sense that it'll reach the top in terms of 5G users. (Para. 1)

翻译：在创新驱动发展战略的指导下，中国在科技领域的投入居于世界领先地位，也正因如此，中国得以在人工智能、量子通信等关键技术上取得重大进展。

2) It's only a matter of time before you can take advantage of all that 5G will offer in your area. (Para. 3)

翻译：中国迟早会解决芯片问题并取得胜利。

3) Much like every generation before it, 5G aims to make mobile communication faster and more reliable as more and more devices go online. (Para. 4)

翻译：和此前的科技政策一样，创新驱动发展战略同样强调创新是提高综合国力的重要支撑。

4) <u>Unlike in the past, when</u> mobile networks only needed to support cell phones that were just for browsing the web and text messaging, we <u>now have all sorts of</u> bandwidth-demanding devices like our HD-streaming smartphones, smartwatches with data plans, etc. (Para. 5)

翻译：过去，传统通信技术主要关注语音和文字的传输。如今，数据通信技术使我们得以传输图像、视频等多种信息。

5) China Mobile <u>has made</u> 5G <u>available in</u> Beijing, Shanghai, and nearly 50 other cities. (Para. 13)

翻译：中国式现代化为解决人类面临的共同问题提供了中国智慧与中国方案、中国力量。

Ⅲ Discourse Practice

1. In the following passage you will learn lots of typical expressions showing comparison and contrast. Complete the passage by choosing the right expressions from the box below. Then read through the passage after you complete it as you will find the expressions and analysis useful in the Produce section.

A. fundamentally different from	B. much smaller than	C. like never before
D. a better response time	E. differences	F. you've never experienced before
G. where 4G fails at	H. the stark differences in	I. although
J. while	K. one underlying difference is	L. faster than
M. it's nothing compared with 5G		

How Are 4G and 5G Different?

Many 4G users are considering buying a cell phone that can support 5G, which has been gaining attraction since 2019. Then what are the actual 1) _____ between the cellular network technology 4G and the newer 5G? Which has been gaining attraction since 2019? 5G is newer, so it has to be better than 4G, right? It is indeed, but how, and what are the specifics? Let's find out.

5G Works Differently from 4G

A new type of mobile network wouldn't be new if it wasn't, in some way, 2) _____ existing ones. 3) _____ 5G's use of unique radio frequencies to achieve what 4G networks cannot.

The radio spectrum is broken up into bands, each with unique features as you move up into higher frequencies. 4G uses frequencies below 6 GHz 4) _____ some 5G networks use higher frequencies like around 30 GHz or more.

These high frequencies are great for a number of reasons, one of the most important being that they support a huge capacity for fast data. Not only are they less cluttered with existing cellular data, and so can be used in the future for increasing bandwidth demands, they're also highly directional and can be used right next to other wireless signals without causing interference.

This is very different from 4G towers that fire data in all directions, potentially wasting both energy and power to beam radio waves at locations that aren't even requesting access to the Internet.

Like 4G, 5G also uses shorter wavelengths, which means that antennas can be 5) _____ existing antennas while still providing precise directional control. Since one base station can utilize even more directional antennas, it means that 5G can support over 1,000 more devices per meter than what's supported by 4G.

5G Is a Lot Faster than 4G

Both 4G and 5G mean speed when they were first launched, but while many love what that 4G speed means, 6) _____ . From a peak speed[1] perspective, 5G is 20 times 7) _____ 4G. This means that during the time it took to

---

1　Theoretically, peak speed could be experienced by a device when there are very few other devices or interferences to affect the speed under ideal conditions.

download just one piece of data with 4G (like a movie), the same could have been downloaded 20 times over a 5G network. So 5G means massively high-speed downloads and uploads—you'll be able to download movies in seconds—and the kind of social media sharing 8) _____

What Can 5G Do that 4G Can't?

Given 9) _____ how they perform, it's clear that 5G is paving a new road to the future for mobile devices and communication, but what does that really mean to you?

It means little latency. Latency is basically the technical term for delay. Less latency means 10) _____ between sending and receiving data. It's the difference between asking your device to do something and it happening. This is big for devices such as cameras, drones, and industrial equipment that relies on 5G, but it's also great news for gamers. It means gaming can be even more mobile. You're not just stuck on a Wi-Fi network, you can game on the go, and do it well. 5G is so fast that everything you do on the Internet now that seems relatively quick might even appear to be instant.

You'll find that you can connect more of your devices to the Internet at the same time without bandwidth issues. 5G at home lets you connect your smartphone, wireless thermostat, video game console, smart locks, virtual reality headset, wireless security cameras, tablet, and laptop all to the same router without worrying that they'll stop working when they're all on at the same time. 11) _____ providing all the data needs to a growing number of mobile devices, 5G opens the airwaves for more Internet-enabled tech like smart traffic lights, wireless sensors, mobile wearables, and car-to-car communication.

12) _____ the evolution of 1G to 4G network was mainly about optimizing wireless network technology and perfect our smartphone, 5G's aspirations are too big to be contained to the world of smartphones alone. Access to the 5G spectrum is not just about faster download speeds for our streaming needs, but about becoming the bridge for the Internet, cloud, and distributed computing industries to build a connected economy 13) _____ .

Produce

Write a Compare-and-Contrast Essay on 4G and 5G

Ⅰ Recap of the Previous Sessions

In Pretest, you've learned the development of the Internet and its applications in China. In Prepare/Probe, you've gained a basic understanding of 5G developments and plans in China. In Practice, you've grasped the key expressions and terms in the text, expressions showing comparison and contrast, and the key information about features of 5G. Now it's time to consider the writing of a compare-and-contrast essay on 4G and 5G.

Ⅱ Definition of a Compare-and-Contrast Essay

Compare-and-contrast essays do just what they say. They identify the similarities and differences between two subjects. Typically, the subjects fall under the same category. For example, you might compare and contrast two different mobile phone brands or two different tourist attractions in the same country.

Ⅲ Procedures of Writing a Compare-and-Contrast Essay

1. Explore similarities and differences

Working out an outline is an essential step before drafting an essay. But, with a compare-and-contrast essay in particular, it's helpful to start with a good old-fashioned list. Take a sheet of paper, draw a vertical line down the center, and list the similarities and differences between the two subjects. When you are listing, you may read through the passage of this unit again to summarize the main similarities and differences. And the passage "How Are 4G and 5G Different?" in the Discourse Practice may also serve as a source of inspiration.

From the passage "When Is 5G Coming to China?" you may learn that both 4G and 5G are wireless technologies. They both empower mobile Internet, operate on radio spectrum frequencies, and connect devices to the Internet. Moreover, they both aim to make mobile communication faster and more reliable as more and more devices go online. Besides, from the passage you may infer that China boasts fast development in both 4G and 5G. You may write down those points first and then search for more information to support them. And you may learn that the differences lie in radio spectrum frequencies, capacity, latency (delay), speed, and reliability. From the passage "How Are 4G and 5G Different?" in the Discourse Practice, you may collect more evidence for each category. Then you may develop a list this way:

4G vs. 5G	
Similarities	**Differences**
• _____ • _____ • _____ • _____ • _____ • _____ • _____	• _____ • _____ • _____ • _____ • _____ • _____

2. **Hone your argument list**

A nice, long list is helpful because you can never know too much about your subject! Now, it's time to pull out your highlighter and hone the most significant elements. Ask yourself among all the elements which ones would interest readers the most. Imagine yourself as the user and not as the developer. 4G and 5G are different on many fronts, and for users, maybe they care more about the differences in speed, delays, and capacity. And they care more about the differences than the similarities. So you may decide to devote one paragraph to similarities while leaving more space for differences.

3. **Gather supporting evidence**

Once you've outlined the main points, you'll need to find evidence for your arguments. Based on the lists you generated, read through the passages again to find the evidence for your comparisons and contrasts.

4. **Decide on the structure**

There are several ways to organize a compare-and-contrast essay. Which one you choose depends on what works best for your ideas.

- Subject by subject. This organization deals with all of the points about Topic A, and then all of the points of Topic B. This style of writing can be helpful if you are using one subject as a "lens" through which to examine the other.

Similarities	Both 4G and 5G are...
Differences (Subject by subject)	4G A. speed B. capacity C. reliability 5G A. speed B. capacity C. reliability

- Point by point. This type of organization switches back and forth between points. For example, you can first discuss the prices of frozen pizza vs. homemade pizza, then the quality of ingredients, and then the convenience factor. The advantage of this type is that it shows very clear what you're comparing and contrasting. The disadvantage is that you switch back and forth between topics, so you need to make sure that you use transitions and signposts to lead your readers through your argument.

Similarities	Both 4G and 5G are...
Differences (Point by point)	The first difference is speed. A. 4G B. 5G The second difference is capacity. A. 4G B. 5G

Ⅳ Organization of a Compare-and-Contrast Essay

Depending on length requirements, most essays include three parts: P1 (Introduction), P2 (Body), and P3 (Conclusion). Compare-and-contrast essays are also composed of the three parts, but they tend to be rich in content.

P1: Introduction

Your introductory paragraph is going to introduce the two subjects to the readers and note why you've chosen to compare and contrast the two. Use a natural way to begin your essay. You may begin your essay by starting with China's 5G launch this way:

_____

_____

P2: Body

Next, you'll move on to the body of the essay. There will be approximately three (or more) paragraphs focusing on key similarities and key differences, with one paragraph devoting to one point.

Remember to use strong transitional words to flow from one point to another. You'll then want to proofread and revise your essay accordingly.

The table below offers the most commonly used connectors in a compare-and-contrast essay:

Similarities	Differences
both; at the same time; correspondingly; compared with; in addition; at the same time; in the same way; similarly; same as; likewise	although; even though; conversely; in contrast; meanwhile; however; on the contrary; on the other hand; unlike; nevertheless

You may also refer to the passage in the Discourse Practice to review the expressions for introducing similarities and differences. When explaining the mechanisms, using some terms listed in Theme-Related Words and Expression will make you sound more professional. And don't forget to put into use some useful sentence structures listed in the Sentence Practice.

P3: Conclusion

By this time, your compare-and-contrast essay already has an introductory section and body paragraphs. Now it is the right time to write the conclusion. Luckily, it is the simplest part, but you should still use a proper structure and format.

Here is what your conclusion can be:

• Summary of key points. Start with a brief discussion of the chosen topics and the main points of your essay. Here you may synthesize the thesis statement with main paragraphs.

• Evaluation. You need to give a brief analysis of the aspects you have discussed in your essay. You should also offer possible solutions and make a prognosis. A great idea will motivate readers to conduct further research on the topic.

- Importance. You should not only mention the importance of the general topic, but also explain why it is necessary to compare or contrast various issues. If you think that it is very difficult, don't worry! Just answer the question "What was my aim in reflecting similarities or differences of these items?". Your answer will indicate the importance of the topic.

After you finish the steps above, you may reread the piece and modify your draft. Remember to get a fresh set of eyes to look at it. Look out for any grammatical errors, confusing phrasing, and repetitive ideas. Here are some things to consider before you turn in your essay:

- Avoid bias. Don't use overly negative or defamatory language to show why a subject is unfavorable; use solid evidence to prove your points instead.

- Avoid first-person pronouns unless told otherwise. In some cases, your teacher may encourage you to use "I" and "you" in your essay. However, if the assignment or your teacher doesn't mention it, stick with third-person instead, like "one may see" or "people may enjoy". This is common practice for formal academic essays.

- Proofread! Spelling and punctuation errors happen to everyone, but not catching them can make you seem lazy. Go over your essay carefully, and ask a friend for help if you're not confident in your own proofreading skills.

Post-Learning Evaluation

No.	Statements	Strongly agree	Agree	Not sure	Disagree	Strongly disagree
1	I have grasped expressions related to the theme.					
2	I am familiar with the key words and phrases in the passage.					
3	I am familiar with the major points of the passage.					
4	I am familiar with the terms explained in the footnotes.					

Continued

No.	Statements	Strongly agree	Agree	Not sure	Disagree	Strongly disagree
5	I am able to present similarities and differences in a clear and logical manner.					
6	I am familiar with the connectors frequently used in compare-and-contrast essays.					
7	I am familiar with the structure of a compare-and-contrast essay.					
8	I am able to write a compare-and-contrast essay when assigned to.					
9	I am able to present the similarities and differences between 4G and 5G.					
10	I have improved my teamwork and collaboration skills in finishing the tasks together with my team members.					
11	I have a better understanding of how the Internet boosts connectivity in China.					
12	I am aware that the 5G plans of various Chinese companies are capturing the attention of overseas institutions and organizations.					
13	As a cutting-edge technology beneficiary, I am aware of how the application of the new generation of technology in China facilitates Chinese people's life.					
14	I take pride in China's rapid development in the new generation of Internet technology.					
15	I am more motivated to tell China's technology innovation story in my own way to international friends.					

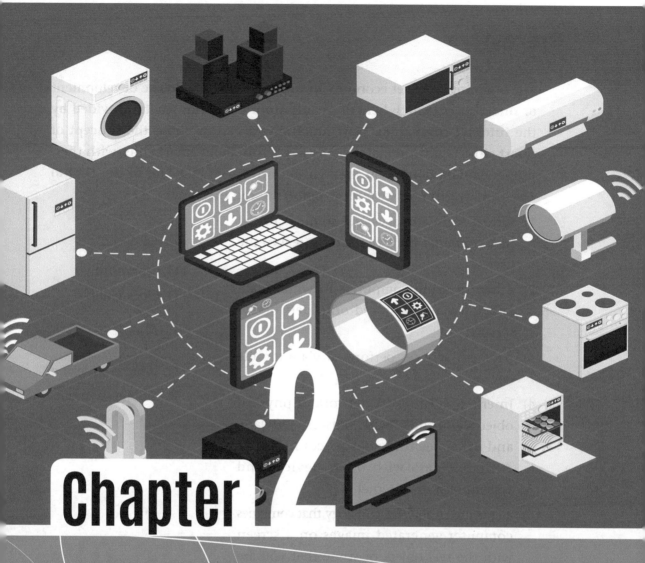

Chapter 2
China's Internet Enterprises

Pretest

The booming Internet economy in China has facilitated the development of smart cities, which benefit greatly from the connectivity provided by the Internet companies. How much do you know about the concept of smart cities? Can you match some key terms about smart cities with their proper explanations? You may go to our MOOC (5.4 Life in the Digital Age—Smart City) to learn more before taking this quiz.

1) virtual reality, images and sounds created by a computer that seem almost real to the user

2) a way of using computers in which data and software are stored on a network of servers

3) payment services performed via a mobile device

4) Internet of Things, a network of physical objects embedded with sensors, software, and other technologies to connect and exchange data with other devices and systems over the Internet

5) augmented reality, a technology that combines computer-generated images on a screen with the real object or scene that you are looking at

6) a process of discovering patterns in large data sets involving methods of machine learning, statistics, and database systems

7) information and communications technology, an extensional term for information technology that stresses the role of unified communications and the integration of telecommunications

8) a growing list of records, called blocks, that are linked using cryptography

(　) A. AR
(　) B. IoT
(　) C. data mining
(　) D. block chain
(　) E. VR
(　) F. ICT
(　) G. cloud computing
(　) H. mobile payment

Pretask

You are currently working as an intern of the Internet Society of China (ISC), and your team leader would like you to write a conference notice about business model innovation of Internet enterprises. What information do you think should be included?

1) To accomplish the task, I plan to take the following steps:

   _____.

   For the first step, I think _____

   might be challenging.

   For the second step, I think _____

   might be challenging.

   _____

   _____

2) I expect to achieve the following goals after learning the unit:

   _____

   _____

Passage

Behind the Fall and Rise of China's Xiaomi

This article is adapted from David Kline's article from WIRED[1] (December, 2019). It introduces Xiaomi's unusual business model which contributed this corporation's rise from its debacle and constructed a passionate user fan base with sustainable bonds.

stumble /ˈstʌmbl/
v. to walk or move in an unsteady way
unprecedented /ʌnˈpresɪdentɪd/
adj. that has never happened, been done or been known before
wither /ˈwɪðə(r)/
v. to become less or weaker, especially before disappearing completely
relentless /rɪˈlentləs/
adj. not stopping; not getting less strong
debacle /dɪˈbɑːkl/
n. an event or a situation that is a complete failure and causes embarrassment

1   Chinese smartphone maker Xiaomi was once the world's most valuable startup. Then it **stumbled**. Now, Xiaomi is clawing its way back.

2   What accounts for the company's **unprecedented** turnaround? Is Xiaomi's renewed success sustainable, or will it **wither** under the **relentless** margin pressures of the phone business? To find the answers to these questions, we have to go back to Xiaomi's 2015–2016 **debacle**, which saw smartphone sales decline to a rumored 41 million in 2016, from a reported 70 million a year earlier. Supply-chain problems associated with the company's rapid growth forced Xiaomi to retreat from several overseas markets. There were organizational problems as well, prompting the restructuring of the smartphone hardware, R&D, supply chain, and quality-management teams. But

---

1   *WIRED* magazine, launched in 1993, covers the tech industry such as Internet and digital culture, science, and security. It is rated Left-Center biased in wording and report choices and factually high due to proper sourcing. These sources are generally trustworthy for information, but may require further investigation.

perhaps the biggest source of Xiaomi's troubles was its exclusive reliance on online sales, which left it unable to reach millions of less tech-**savvy** customers in China's smaller cities and rural areas.

savvy /'sævi/
adj. having practical knowledge and understanding of sth.; having common sense

3   In a classic case of "turning a bad thing into a good thing", however, Xiaomi used its near-fatal stumble to fashion a radical new business model. With sales rebounding, and the company expanding globally, it's worth examining the inner workings of that unusual model, and how it helped to power the company's remarkable **resurgence**.

resurgence /rɪ'sɜːdʒəns/
n. the return and growth of an activity that had stopped

4   Like many businesses in the Internet age, Xiaomi had initially relied on a dual business model of selling hardware products and online services.[2] Most revenue came from the sale of affordable phones and smart TVs, which serve as platforms for Xiaomi's online services. The hardware products have razor-thin profit margins, so most of Xiaomi's profits came from the online services. These include hundreds of thousands of hours of movies and shows—available à la carte or via an all-you-can-eat $7.50 monthly fee—as well as games and other offerings. Xiaomi even operates a profitable online service offering small loans to Xiaomi phone users **vetted** with the help of a sophisticated artificial-intelligence engine to assess creditworthiness.

vet /vet/
v. to check the contents, quality, etc. of sth. carefully

Ecosystem Strategy[3]

5   **In the wake of** Xiaomi's **setback**, company executives concluded they needed a third leg to

in the wake of coming after or following sb./sth.

setback /'setbæk/
n. a difficulty or problem that delays or prevents sth., or makes a situation worse

---

2 Now, Xiaomi's business model comprises of three parts that are closely connected: hardware, Internet services, and new retail. Xiaomi describes this business model as a "triathlon model".

3 Xiaomi's ecosystem strategy is a marriage of funding and incubation for startups. Based on ecosystem strategy, a large network centered on Xiaomi's core products was constructed: smartphones and smart hardware products.

ecosystem /'iːkəʊsɪstəm/
n. all the plants and
living creatures
in a particular
area considered
in relation to
their physical
environment

their business model—offline retail stores. But they wanted the stores to go beyond selling phones to forge sustainable bonds with customers. Their solution is to create an **ecosystem** of some 100 startups as partners to provide Xiaomi with other Internet-connected home and tech products that would draw customers to its stores.

6 Xiaomi's senior vice president Wang Xiang explained how the ecosystem strategy drives traffic as we sat in his office: "Buying a phone or TV is a low-frequency event. How many times do you need to go back to the store?" he said. "But what if you also need a Bluetooth[4] speaker, an Internet-enabled rice cooker, or the first affordable air purifier in China—and each one of those products is not only best in class, but costs less than the existing products in that category? Our ecosystem even gives customers unusual new products that they never knew existed. So they keep coming back to Xiaomi's Mi Home Store to see what we've got."

7 Wang says the strategy aims to reduce "pain points[5]" for Chinese consumers. He points to air pollution. Quality air purifiers cost roughly $500, he says. So Xiaomi funded a startup with an air-pollution expert, offering help with design and manufacturing, access to its supply chain, and lessons of its own low-cost operating efficiency. The result is the Mi Air Purifier 2, which sells for $105. It's connected to smartphones, allowing users to monitor the air in their homes, and receive alerts when the filter needs changing.

---

4 Bluetooth is a wireless technology standard used for exchanging data between fixed and mobile devices over short distances and building personal area networks.

5 A pain point is a persistent or recurring problem (as with a product or service) that frequently inconveniences or annoys customers.

8   The purifier was a **blockbuster** hit. "Within two months we were the top seller of air purifiers in China," claims Wang. "And that's how we solved the 'pain point' in air purifiers."

9   The company took a similar approach with fitness bands, designing a **streamlined** device with a battery life of almost 60 days that solved the "pain point" of having to recharge the bands every few days. Xiaomi is now the world's top seller of fitness bands, **ahead of** Fitbit[6] and Apple. Ditto for Xiaomi's award-winning power banks, which provide more charges than rivals at a lower price; Xiaomi is the world sales leader in this category as well.

10   All its ecosystem products, from pillows to air purifiers, and from rice cookers to portable Bluetooth 4.0 speakers, aim to resolve similar price-to-performance "pain points" for customers. The products are inexpensive, but not cheaply designed or manufactured. They've won more than 100 international design awards.

11   The strategy has its critics. "When we started with this new model, many people said we were not a focused company," Wang acknowledged. "They said we are like a supermarket, or a department store—that we sell everything and are therefore focused on nothing. 'You're a smartphone company,' they argued. 'Why you do rice cookers? Why you do batteries or pens or luggage? Are you crazy?' But it's not crazy. It works very well for us."

12   Still, it's hard to argue with Xiaomi's numbers.

blockbuster
/'blɒkbʌstə(r)/
n. sth. very successful, especially a very successful book or film

streamline /'striːmlaɪn/
v. to make a system, an organization, etc. work better, especially in a way that saves money

ahead of
further advanced than sb./sth.; in front of sb., for example in a race or competition

---

6 Fitbit, Inc. is an American company headquartered in San Francisco, California. Its products include activity trackers, smartwatches and wireless-enabled wearable technology devices.

shipment /ˈʃɪpmənt/
n. a load of goods that are sent from one place to another

debut /ˈdeɪbjuː/
v. to introduce a product to the public for the first time

ceramic /səˈræmɪk/
n. a pot or other object made of clay that has been made permanently hard by heat

sensor /ˈsensə(r)/
n. a device that can react to light, heat, pressure, etc. in order to make a machine, etc. do sth. or show sth.

interface /ˈɪntəfeɪs/
n. the way a computer program presents information to a user
or receives information from a user, in particular the layout of the screen and the menus

activate /ˈæktɪveɪt/
v. to make sth. such as a device or chemical process start working

Strategy Analytics says Xiaomi's phone **shipments** soared 91 percent in the third quarter—in a market growing only 5 percent annually worldwide. Analysts say Xiaomi's revenues could reach 110 billion yuan, or $17 billion, this year.

13 One big driver of the sales increase is Xiaomi's Mi Mix phone, which was the world's first bezel-less phone when it **debuted** in October 2016. Chief Financial Officer Shou Zi Chew explained the engineering challenge. "In order to get rid of the forehead on the phone and replace it with an edge-to-edge screen, we first had to replace the speaker," he said. "To do this, we put a piece of **ceramic** behind the touchscreen panel that vibrates the sound into your ear." Then Xiaomi used ultrasound in place of a proximity **sensor** to measure the distance between a user's face and the phone, and shrank the front-facing camera to a spot in the bottom corner of the phone. In September, Xiaomi introduced the Mi Mix 2.

14 Xiaomi's "pain point"-solving products have created a passionate fan base at home and abroad. The company's Mi phone user **interface** (called MIUI[7]), the Android-based operating system that runs on Xiaomi smartphones, now has 300 million **activated** users. According to Shou, those users spend close to five hours a day on their phones, helping to explain the near Comic-Con[8] fervor of Mi Fan clubs worldwide.

15 The company taps its fan base to support the business. For example, Xiaomi asks users to suggest

---

7 MIUI is a stock and aftermarket firmware for smartphones and tablet computers developed by Xiaomi.

8 The San Diego Comic Convention (Comic-Con International) is organized for charitable purposes and dedicated to raising the general public's awareness of and appreciation for comics and related popular art forms.

new features, and then lets them vote each week on which to **incorporate** into the operating system. Every Friday at 5 p.m. Beijing time, Xiaomi issues an update to the MIUI that includes the most popular new features.

incorporate
/ɪnˈkɔːpəreɪt/
v. to include sth. so that it forms a part of sth.

The Xiaomi Way

16   Shou recalled one case last year when a user said that he had gotten so drunk one night that he couldn't find the flashlight app on his phone to locate his keys. Could Xiaomi enable it with a long press of the fingerprint sensor? Other fans loved the idea, and now it's part of the MIUI. This **systematized back and forth** may seem like small change in the building of a global business. But it makes customers feel invested in Xiaomi, as if the company belongs to them.

systematize
/ˈsɪstəmətaɪz/
v. to arrange sth. according to a system
back and forth
from one place to another and back again repeatedly

17   So there you have it. "The Xiaomi Way" is a kind of democratized, grass-roots business model that relies on a passionate user fan base to co-design the phone UI and **evangelize** products developed by a network of startup partners. To Xiaomi executives, the result is a Costco[9]-style degree of loyalty and brand "stickiness" among customers.

evangelize
/ɪˈvændʒəlaɪz/
v. to try to persuade people to become Christians

18   Wang, the senior vice president, acknowledges that Xiaomi faces many challenges. Among the most prominent is global expansion, especially into the high-stakes U.S. market, which Wang believes will occur "by 2019" but some think may come sooner. "This is a very attractive market for us," he said. "My ultimate goal is to be a strong player in the U.S. market."

---

9   Costco Wholesale Corporation is an American multinational corporation which operates a chain of membership-only warehouse clubs. To some customers, going to Costco is like going on a treasure hunt.

arena /əˈriːnə/
n. an area of activity that concerns the public, especially one where there is a lot of opposition between different groups or countries

patent /ˈpætnt/
v. to obtain a special document giving you the right to make or sell a new invention or product

stymie /ˈstaɪmi/
v. to prevent sb. from doing sth. that he/she has planned or wants to do; to prevent sth. from happening

portfolio /pɔːtˈfəʊliəʊ/
n. the range of products or services offered by a particular company or organization

19   Wang knows U.S. customers have high expectations for service, and that most phones in the U.S. are sold through telecom companies, an **arena** where Xiaomi has no experience. "So we will certainly have to work with at least one carrier and hopefully all of them if we can." That will require a lot of engineering resources for a company with barely 14,000 employees. Each carrier has its own requirements for phones to work on its network. "Probably we will have to pick one carrier first, and make that successful," Wang says. "Then the other carriers will come to us, and we'll have more resources to comply with their requirements."

20   Before testing the U.S. market, Xiaomi is expanding in Western Europe, most recently in Spain, where it began selling phones last month. To successfully expand internationally, Xiaomi must secure the global intellectual property rights to the components used in its products, including the **patented** wireless, video and audio technologies employed in smartphones. Without this IP protection, Xiaomi could find itself **stymied** by costly lawsuits, and potentially find its products barred from various markets, as they were for a time in India, thanks to a patent suit filed by Ericsson in 2014.

21   Xiaomi learned from that experience, and has been building its **portfolio** of some 5,700 patents ever since—most generated internally, some acquired from firms like Microsoft[10] and Nokia[11]. If Xiaomi

---

10 Microsoft Corporation is an American multinational technology company that develops, manufactures, licenses, supports, and sells computer software, consumer electronics, and personal computers and services.

11 Nokia Corporation is a Finnish multinational telecommunication, information technology, and consumer electronics company. It is a major contributor to the mobile telephony industry and was once the largest worldwide supplier of mobile phones and smartphones.

doesn't "**gun up**" with the necessary patent protection by the time it launches in the U.S., Apple or another big smartphone player will be eagerly waiting to slap the company with a billion-dollar patent suit.

gun up
to be ready

22   Meanwhile, as Xiaomi continues to expand beyond China, it now sells products in 60 countries. Having already invested $4 billion in its Chinese partner ecosystem, Xiaomi says it will now invest $1 billion in building similar partnerships with 100 startups in India, its largest market outside China. Xiaomi also announced last month a broad strategic partnership with Chinese search giant Baidu to co-develop conversational AI products for the Internet of Things (IoT) market. And it is planning to expand its retail networks both at home and abroad to a total of more than 2,000 branded Mi Home Stores by 2019.

23   No one at Xiaomi believes success is assured. "This is the wrong industry for relaxing," **conceded** Wang. "Competition is very fierce. You can't relax, you can't sleep—and if you do, you keep one eye open. You feel like if you go on vacation for a few weeks, when you come back you will have lost the business."

concede /kən'si:d/
v. to admit that sth. is true, logical, etc. after first denying it or resisting it

(1,873 words)

Theme-Related Words & Expressions

startup	创业公司
supply chain	供应链
hardware	硬件
tech-savvy	精通技术的
à la carte	按菜单点菜
creditworthiness	信誉；信贷价值
offline retail store	线下零售店
Bluetooth speaker	蓝牙扬声器
air purifier	空气净化器
Mi Home Store	小米之家
pain point	痛点
fitness band	运动手环
bezel-less	无边框的
edge-to-edge	边对边；无边框
touchscreen	触摸屏
proximity sensor	近距离传感器
front-facing camera	前置摄像头
activated user	活跃用户
flashlight	闪光灯
fingerprint sensor	指纹传感器
stickiness	（用户）黏性
IoT (Internet of Things)	物联网
retail network	零售网络
patent suit	专利诉讼
New Quality Productive Forces	新质生产力
New Growth Drivers	新动能
Industrial Internet	工业互联网
Internet of Vehicles	车联网
Digital Ecosystem	数字生态
Digital Transformation	数字化转型
Human-machine Interaction	人机交互
AIGC, Artificial Intelligence Generative Content	人工智能生成内容
Intelligent Industry	智能产业
Joint Contribution and Shared Benefits	共建共享

Prepare/Probe

❶ Reading Comprehension

Answer the following questions according to the passage.

1) Why does the author describe Xiaomi in 2015 and 2016 as a "debacle"?

_____

_____

2) What did Xiaomi's executives conclude from the company's setback? What is their solution to Xiaomi's "debacle"?

_____

_____

3) How does the ecosystem strategy drive traffic and work well for Xiaomi?

_____

_____

4) What is "The Xiaomi Way"? How can it create a "Costco-style degree of loyalty and brand 'stickiness' among customers"?

_____

_____

5) What makes a challenge for Xiaomi to enter the U.S. market?

_____

_____

❷ Structure Building

Check your understanding of the overall structure of the passage by completing the following diagram.

Brief Introduction to Xiaomi's Fall and Rise	
The unusual business model contributed to Xiaomi's rise from its debacle. (Paras. 1–4)	**Xiaomi's 2015–2016 debacle** • Smartphone sales 1) _____ to a rumored 41 million in 2016 from 70 million a year earlier. • Supply-chain problems with the company's rapid growth forced Xiaomi to 2) _____ from several overseas markets. • 3) _____ problems prompted the restructuring of the smartphone hardware, R&D, supply chain, and quality-management teams. • Xiaomi's exclusive reliance on 4) _____ is a big trouble. **Turning a bad thing into a good thing** • Sales 5) _____, and the company expanded globally. • Unlike other businesses relying on 6) _____ (hardware products sales and 7) _____ online services), unusual business model helped the company's resurgence.
Xiaomi's Ecosystem Strategy	

The ecosystem strategy effectively helps forge sustainable bonds with customers.
 	
(Paras. 5–15)
	Ecosystem has the following advantages:
	• Providing newer and more products: 8) _____ besides cell phones;
	• Costing 9) _____;
	• Reducing 10) "_____".
	  ■ 11) _____: quality air purifiers cost less.
	  ■ 12) _____: fitness band has a battery life of almost 60 days.
	  ■ 13) _____ screen: get rid of the forehead; Mi Mix phone was introduced.
	Ecosystem products created a passionate fan base
	• The company's Mi phone user interface (called MIUI) has 300 million 14) _____ users.
	• They spend nearly five hours a day on their phones.

Continued

The Xiaomi Way	
"The Xiaomi Way" is a democratized business model that relies on a passionate user fan base. (Paras. 16–18)	• Xiaomi asks users to suggest new features and let them vote on which to 15) _____ into the operating system. • Xiaomi's business model creates a Costco-style degree of loyalty and brand 16) _____ among customers.

Practice

❶ Vocabulary Practice

1. **Match the following theme-related words and expressions in Column A with their Chinese equivalents in Column B.**

Column A	Column B
1) intellectual property	A. 创业公司
2) operating system	B. 活跃用户
3) patent suit	C. 物联网
4) bezel-less	D. 供应链
5) retail network	E. 零售网络
6) revenue	F. 专利诉讼
7) startup	G. 操作系统
8) supply chain	H. 精通技术的
9) tech-savvy	I. 知识产权
10) activated user	J. 无边框的
11) sensor	K. 收益
12) IoT (Internet of Things)	L. 传感器

2. **Group the words and expressions related to Xiaomi. You may find the words and expressions from Exercise 1. Start with the examples given below.**

Xiaomi's customers	tech-savvy; _____
Xiaomi's products	sensor; _____
Business terms	supply chain; _____

3. **Fill in the blanks with the words in the box. Change the form if necessary.**

incorporate	unprecedented	relentless	setback	shipment
debut	sensor	patent	passionate	blockbuster

1) We believe Xiaomi's _____ in 2016 is unlikely to happen again, as it has a more mature offline distribution network and reliable supply chain than before.

2) Xiaomi's Mi 11 is a real _____. In 21 days, more than one million pieces were sold.

3) If you're _____ about IT and electronics, buy Xiaomi's Mi Mix Alpha.

4) MIUI 12.5 promises to improve system performance by around 25 percent and _____ new themes, wallpapers and much more.

5) A month after it _____ in China, MIUI 12 has made its way to the global scene.

6) Xiaomi applied for 2,318 _____ in 2014, and Lei plans to get tens of thousands more in the coming years.

7) Xiaomi showed a(n) _____ concept of the phone. Is this the future of mobile phones?

8) Goods are packed before being transported to the docks for _____ overseas.

9) Xiaomi consistently focuses on sales promotion like a(n) _____ machine.

10) A smartphone _____ is the device installed on a user's phone to gather data for various user purposes.

Ⅱ Sentence Practice

Study the sentence structure first, and then translate each of the given Chinese sentences into English by imitating the sentence structure.

1) <u>There were</u> organizational problems <u>as well</u>, <u>prompting</u> the restructuring of the smartphone hardware, R&D, supply chain, and quality-management teams. (Para. 2)

翻译：产业变革的趋势同样存在，并促使传统媒体行业进行数字化转型。

_____

_____

2) In a classic case of "turning a bad thing into a good thing", however, Xiaomi <u>used</u> its near-fatal stumble <u>to fashion</u> a radical new business model. (Para. 3)

翻译：随着新一代人工智能的发展，各大互联网企业纷纷尝试采用深度学习技术，创建涵盖文字、语音、代码、图像、视频的生成式人工智能模型。

_____

_____

3) <u>In the wake of</u> Xiaomi's setback, company executives concluded they needed a third leg to their business model—offline retail stores. (Para. 5)

翻译：随着创新在经济发展中的主导作用日益凸显，新质生产力得以从传统的生产力发展路径中解放出来。

_____

_____

4) Xiaomi funded a startup with an air-pollution expert, <u>offering help with</u> design and manufacturing, <u>access to</u> its supply chain, and lessons of its own low-cost operating efficiency. (Para. 7)

翻译：中国的互联网产业稳步发展，助力了实体经济的数字化转型，也为实施创新驱动发展战略提供了路径。

_____

_____

5) The company took a similar approach with fitness bands, designing a streamlined device with a battery life of almost 60 days that solved the "pain point" of having to recharge the bands every few days. (Para. 9)

翻译：中国的生态文明建设也在数字化、智能化领域采用了类似的做法，以构建美丽中国数字化治理体系。

_____

_____

⊞ Discourse Practice

Complete the fragments with the suitable words or phrases in the box, and then sequence the fragments in the correct order. You may not use any of the words or phrases more than once.

although	beyond	therefore	initially
still	amid	at its low point	such as

A. The smartphone maker began to play on the offensive with investments in hundreds of startups, aiming to build out a physical retail presence _____ the scope of smartphone sales.

B. Its hundreds of products, _____ branded scooters, chargers, air purifiers, suitcases, and smartphones, work as platforms for services such as cloud storage, while also providing a monthly subscription for thousands of hours of TV shows, movies, games, and other offerings.

C. The strategy has its critics. "When we started with this new model, many people said we were not a focused company," said Wang Xiang, Xiaomi's senior vice president, in an interview with *WIRED*. "They said we are like a supermarket, or a department store—that we sell everything and are _____ focused on nothing."

D. _____ Xiaomi has already overcome significant challenges in recent years as it has essentially resurrected its phone sales and other business, there are always new threats.

E. _____, it's hard to argue with Xiaomi's numbers. Strategy Analytics says Xiaomi's phone shipments soared 91 percent in the third quarter—in a market growing only 5 percent annually worldwide. Analysts say Xiaomi's revenues could reach 110 billion yuan, or $17 billion, this year.

F. _____, Xiaomi had funded itself on selling hardware products and online services, like many of its peers in the Internet age. The company generated a bulk of its revenue from lower-margin device sales, while the majority of its profits came from its online service business.

G. _____ in 2016, Xiaomi saw smartphone sales decline to 41 million, down from a reported 70 million in 2016, according to the IDC.

H. The goal was to create an ecosystem of partner startups offering a diverse range of Internet-connected home and tech products, working to drive foot traffic at brick-and-mortar locations.

I. _____ Xiaomi's roughest times, management decided to add a third leg to create the company's unique business model.

J. Its billionaire founder, who has been dubbed "the Steve Jobs of China", decided his company would sell much more than smartphones.

Sequence: _____

Produce

Write a Conference Notice About Business Model Innovation of Internet Enterprises

❶ Recap of the Previous Sessions

In Pretest, you've gained a basic understanding of smart cities. In Prepare/Probe, you've grasped the main idea and structure of Xiaomi's business model. In Practice, you've familiarized yourself with the necessary language points, sentence patterns, and the key information needed for Produce. Now it's time to consider the production of a conference notice.

❷ Definition of a Conference Notice

A conference notice sometimes overlaps with the call for papers in content. However, it is a formal way to inform the concerned parties and participants of details and requirements of the conference, such as major topics to be discussed, specific requirements, registration, accommodation, etc.

Different Kinds of Meetings

Meeting is a general term for various kinds of assembly of people for a particular purpose. It can mean any of gathering, pre-arranged, formal or informal. To specifically clarify a meeting, therefore, the names of different meetings should be further demarcated.

1. Conference

A conference often covers multiple themes or topics within a field, and may bring together inter-disciplinary scholars and practitioners.

2. Symposium

A symposium generally has a much narrower focus than a research or academic conference. Often an event like this will cover just one topic, so a symposium is often smaller and shorter than an average conference.

3. Congress

The basic characteristic of a congress is that it is usually attended by representatives or delegates who belong to national or international, governmental or non-governmental organizations.

4. Convention

A convention is a kind of routine meeting, at which a large gathering of people meet and discuss the business of their organization or political group.

5. Forum

A forum is a discussion group, where ideas related to a subject under discussion can be raised and evaluated on a (more-or-less) equal and informal basis.

6. Seminar

A seminar is usually a class-like meeting, where participants discuss a particular topic or subject that is presented by several major speakers. A seminar can be taken as lecturing plus discussion—the discussion being a follow-up of the lecturing.

7. Workshop

Workshop refers to a period of discussion or practical work on a particular subject, in which a group of people learn about the subject by sharing their knowledge or experience.

8. Colloquium

Colloquium is sometimes a formal word for seminar. It is usually a large academic seminar like panel discussion. Colloquia are usually attended by certain invited experts or professionals in a particular field.

Ⅳ Format of a Conference Notice

A conference notice may include but not be limited to the following information:

1. General information

The general information of a conference, which needs to be familiarized by a conference participant, can be very comprehensive. Usually, the conference participant should know the meeting's name, date, location, topics for discussion, time of arrival, accommodations, weather conditions, and even the local temperature and recommendations for clothing. It may also include information about activities before, during, and after the conference.

1) Name of the meeting

Each conference has a formal name, for example, "American Academy of Physicists in Medicine 25th Annual Meeting". Besides, in the conference notice or other documents, the short term for the formal name may be used. For example, the short term for the conference name above is "AAPM's 25th Annual Meeting".

2) Date

The announcement should include the starting and ending date of the conference. For example, you may state that the symposium is held from July 7 to 13, 2021.

3) Location/Venue

International conferences are usually held in places boasting of extensive scientific, educational and academic activities, such as specialized centers of international exchanges and cooperation at universities or research institutes, often with available accommodations, telecommunication facilities, convenient transportation and beautiful scenery.

The following are some useful expressions for conference date and location:

- The 10th IEEE/CIC International Conference on Communications in China will be held in Xiamen, China, 28–30 July, 2021.
- The workshop is to be held on Friday, March 21, 2021 from 12 noon to 5 p.m. at the Marden Conference Center at Clemson University.

4) Theme

Theme of the meeting is the central idea that runs through the whole meeting.

The following are some useful expressions for conference theme:

- The workshop, including panel discussion and breakout brainstorming sessions, will focus on four key topics.
- Themed "Connecting Cultures Around the Globe", the flagship conference of the IEEE Communications Society will feature a comprehensive high-quality technical program including 12 symposia, selected areas in communications track and a variety of tutorials and workshops.

5) Topics of interest

Topics of interest refer to the focused areas of the conference.

6) Objectives

Objectives of the meeting are the targets to be achieved in the meeting.

7) Accommodation (hotel, cost, reservation, etc.)

Conference organizer provides a selection of hotels for the participants. Participants can choose the hotels offered by them or find hotels themselves.

2. Paper submission information

The paper submission information of a conference is instructive and informative, which includes:

1) Topics: e.g. EMNLP 2021 has the goal of a broad technical program. Relevant topics for the conference include, but are not limited to, the following areas...

2) Abstract: the deadline, length, and format of the abstract.

3) Full text: the deadline, length, style sheet, photocopies of the paper, and other detailed requirements.

4) Authorship: e.g. the author list for submissions should include all (and only) individuals who made substantial contributions to the work presented. Each author listed on a submission to EMNLP 2021 will be notified of submissions, revisions and the final decision. No changes to the order or composition of authorship may be made to submissions to EMNLP 2021 after the abstract submission deadline.

3. Organizational information

The organizational information is necessary, including information about the sponsors, organizers, organizing committee and many other committees as well.

1) Conference sponsor

Generally speaking, the sponsor of a conference is the institution that initiates the conference. As a rule, the sponsor of a conference is a financial supporter for the conference.

2) Conference organizer

An organizer of a conference is the one who actually organizes the conference. The organizer is usually entrusted by the sponsor to organize the conference.

3) Organizing committee

For a large-scale conference, the organizing committee is usually a rather large body that consists of the chairperson, vice chairpersons, the secretary general, deputy secretary generals, and other committee members. Each of them is in charge of a specific part of the organizing work and is responsible to the sponsors and organizers. Take IEEE/CIC International Conference on Communications in China, 2021 as an example. The committee includes General Co-Chairs, Technical Program Co-Chairs, Publicity Co-Chairs, Invited Track Co-Chairs, Industry Committee Co-Chairs, System Demo Co-Chairs, Workshop Co-Chairs, Tutorial Co-Chairs, Panel Co-Chairs, Publication Chair, Local Organizing Committee Chair.

The following are useful expressions for the organizing committee:

- The Center for Asia-Pacific Initiatives is hosting this unique conference and looks forward to welcoming conference participants to the University of Victoria.

- The Ministry of Water Resources of China, the International Association of Hydrologic Science, and more than 10 international and national organizations will sponsor this conference.

4. Participants information

The participants information is important for the conference attendees. This kind of information usually includes the number of participants, the requirements for attendances and the conference "VIPs" as well.

1) Number of participants

This information includes the expected number of the participants, which indicates the scale of a conference.

2) Requirements for attendances

Conference sponsors set restrictions on the participants of a conference. Conference announcement gives specific requirements, such as membership, age and specialization, for the participants.

3) Specially invited and plenary (keynote) speakers

Specially invited and plenary (keynote) speakers are the so-called "VIPs", the important figures present at the conference, including but not limited to the members of academic committees, and leading figures in the fields. The information about these people is useful to all the participants for further communication.

5. Conference program information

The available conference program information should include the program schedule and registration.

1) Program schedule

Conference program schedule serves as a guide as well as a plan for the participants. It lists a series of activities to be done at a definite time and place. It helps participants fulfill their activities in accordance with the plan. Usually it contains the following information: time, date(s), activities, place, and people involved.

The following are useful expressions for a program schedule:

- The conference will be held at the University of Victoria, Victoria, B.C, Canada, August 22–24, 2016.
- The workshop is to be held on Friday, March 21, 2016 from 12 noon to 5

p.m. at the Marden Conference Center at Clemson University.

2) Registration

Registration for the meeting must be made beforehand by sending Conference Registration Form via mail or email. The registration part might include the registration date, types of registration (e.g. author conference registration, conference registration, and workshop only registration), registration fees, etc.

6. Contact information

Contact information, such as name (first and last), phone number, email address and website, should be included to provide participants with more information about the program or registration.

The following are useful expressions for contact information:

- Please go to www.scepscor.org/outreach/workshop to access the tentative agenda, to register, and to request a travel grant to attend.

- Questions regarding to the conference and registration should be directed to Ms. Wang, wanglili@caac.com, or by telephoning (8610) 67554675.

Ⅴ Samples of Conference Notices

Sample 1:

The 4th CCF Conference on Natural Language Processing & Chinese Computing (NLPCC 2015)

Theme: Natural Language Analysis and Understanding in Big Data

The conference on Natural Language Processing and Chinese Computing (NLPCC) is the annual meeting of the CCF TCCI (Technical Committee of Chinese Information, China Computer Federation). NLPCC is a leading international conference specialized in the fields of Natural Language Processing (NLP) and Chinese Computing (CC). It serves as a main forum for researchers and practitioners from academia, industry, and government to share their ideas, research results and experiences, and to promote their research and technical innovations in the fields. Previous NLPCC conferences were successfully held in Beijing (2012), Chongqing (2013), and Shenzhen (2014).

Today, NLP and CC technologies are among the most active research and development areas due to the rapid advancement of the Internet as well as the worldwide proliferation of mobile devices and social media. The fields are facing many new challenges arisen from intelligent applications and big data, such as business intelligence, social analytics, etc. The fourth conference of NLPCC will focus on Natural Language Analysis and Understanding in Big Data, including Fundamental Research in Language Computing, Multi-Lingual Access, Web Mining / Text Mining, Machine Learning for NLP, Knowledge Graph, NLP for Social Network, Information Retrieval, Question & Answering as well as the Applications of Language Computing.

Important Dates

- Submission Deadline: June 19, 2015 (23:59, Beijing time)
- Tutorials / CCF Advanced Disciplines Lectures (ADL): October 9–11, 2015
- Main Conference: October 12–13

Conference Venue

Treasure Palace Hotel, Nanchang, China.

Call for Papers

NLPCC 2015 welcomes original technical papers on new concepts, innovative research, systems, standards, testing & evaluation, applications, and industrial case studies related to NLP & CC. Authors are invited to submit complete and unpublished papers in English or in Chinese. Papers currently under review in other conferences or journals are acceptable; yet commitment to the conference must be made upon acceptance.

Relevant topics of NLPCC 2015 include, but are not limited to, the following:

- Fundamentals of Language Computing
- Word Segmentation & Named Entity Recognition
- Syntactic Parsing, Semantic Analysis & Discourse Analysis
- NLP for Minority and Low-resource Languages
- Applications of Natural Language Processing
- Digital Publishing, Document Engineering, OCR & Fonts Computing
- NLP for Mobile Computing

Submission Guidelines

English submissions should follow the LNCS formatting instructions, without exceeding twelve (12) pages. The submissions must therefore be formatted in accordance with the standard Springer style sheets ([LaTeX][1] [Microsoft Word]) and should be no more than 12 pages in length. Submissions in Chinese should follow the formatting instructions of the *ACTA Scientiarum Naturalium Universitatis Pekinensis*[2] [Format Template], without exceeding eight (8) pages in A4 (210 × 297 mm) size.

Manuscripts should be submitted electronically through the submission website. Email submissions will not be considered. Authors of Chinese submissions are required to provide Chinese titles in the submission system. All student first authors are encouraged to contact nlpcc@pku.edu.cn, indicating their names, affiliations, and the titles of their submissions.

Registration

Please visit the following website and register at NLPCC 2015.

Registration website: http://59.108.48.38/nlpcc2015/index.php

Keynote Speakers

- Professor Dan Roth, UIUC

  Keynote topic: Learning and Inference for Natural Language Understanding

- Professor Jian-Yun Nie, University of Montreal

  Keynote topic: The Role of NLP in IR

Accommodations

NLPCC 2015 recommends the following hotels. You can also reserve other hotels by yourself.

- Treasure Palace Hotel

  Address: No. 125, Torch Street, High Tech District, Nanchang, Jiangxi

- Maison de Bonheur Hotel

---

1 LaTeX is a typesetting system designed for the production of technical and scientific documentation. The writer uses markup tagging conventions to define the general structure of a document, to stylize text throughout a document, and to add citations and cross-references.

2 *ACTA Scientiarum Naturalium Universitatis Pekinensis* is a comprehensive academic journal started in 1955 sponsored by Peking University. The journal publishes original research articles and literature reviews in natural sciences and technical sciences.

Address: No. 719, Torch Street, High Tech District, Nanchang, Jiangxi

Organizing Committee

Organizer: China Computer Federation (CCF)

Host: State Key Lab of Digital Publishing Technology

Sponsor: Microsoft Research, Sougou, Inc., MingBo Digital Education

For more information, please visit http://tcci.ccf.org.cn/conference/2015/index.html.

Sample 2:

ACL-IJCNLP 2021: The Joint Conference of the 59th Annual Meeting of the Association for Computational Linguistics and the 10th International Joint Conference on Natural Language Processing

The Joint Conference of the 59th Annual Meeting of the Association for Computational Linguistics and the 10th International Joint Conference on Natural Language Processing (ACL-IJCNLP 2021) is currently scheduled to take place in Bangkok, Thailand, during August 1–6, 2021. We are monitoring the ongoing global pandemic and will update the conference plans (e.g., moving to a virtual or hybrid format) as needed closer to the conference dates.

ACL-IJCNLP 2021 invites the submission of long and short papers on substantial, original, and unpublished research in all aspects of Computational Linguistics and Natural Language Processing. This preliminary call for papers will be updated with more details in the first full call for papers and more details will be available on the conference website.

ACL-IJCNLP 2021 has the goal of a broad technical program. Relevant topics for the conference include, but are not limited to, the following areas:

- Computational Social Science and Social Media
- Dialogue and Interactive Systems
- Discourse and Pragmatics
- Ethics and NLP

Following the previous conferences, ACL-IJCNLP 2021 will be open for two types of submissions: long and short papers. Author guidelines will be published at the conference webpage.

The submission site is now available at https://www.softconf.com/acl2021/demos/. Please be aware of the paper submission deadline on March 25, 2021.

Now you can write a conference notice based on the following information in reference to the two samples.

Name	The International Conference on International Business (ICIB 2021)
Organizer	Internet Society of China (ISC)
Theme	Innovative Management Practices for Sustainable Business Models
Date	February 25–26, 2021
Location	China National Convention Center No.7 Tianchen East Road, Chaoyang District, Beijing, China, 100105
Keynote speaker	Professor Dan Ross
Accommodation	Building 1, China National Convention Center Grand Hotel, No. 8 Precinct, Beichen West Road, Chaoyang District, Beijing, China
Keynote topic	Xiaomi—The Internet Way
Registration	www.icib2021.org
Contact	ICIB2021@163.com, 010-3336666

Post-Learning Evaluation

No.	Statements	Strongly agree	Agree	Not sure	Disagree	Strongly disagree
1	I have grasped the expressions related to the theme.					
2	I am familiar with the key words and phrases in the passage.					

Continued

No.	Statements	Strongly agree	Agree	Not sure	Disagree	Strongly disagree
3	I am familiar with the major points of the passage.					
4	I am familiar with the terms explained in the footnotes.					
5	I am familiar with the major types of meetings.					
6	I am familiar with the expressions about information organization in a conference notice.					
7	I know the formats of a conference notice.					
8	I am able to write a conference notice when assigned to.					
9	I understand my role in the accomplishment of the project, and I have improved my teamwork skills through peer interaction.					
10	I will form a more critical view towards the Western coverage on Chinese Internet enterprises, and if there are some misunderstandings, I would like to explain.					
11	I will share my view with international friends if they have any misunderstanding about Chinese Internet enterprises.					
12	I take pride in Chinese Internet enterprises' rapid advances in business model innovation.					
13	I appreciate Chinese entrepreneurs' innovation efforts.					
14	After learning this chapter, I will tell the story of Chinese Internet enterprises' business innovation to international friends when I have the opportunity.					

Chapter **3**

Chinese Lifestyle in Internet Plus Era

Pretest

Match the key points of digital payments with their proper explanations.

1) the process of coordinating and moving resources such as people, materials, inventory, and equipment—from one location to storage at the desired destination

2) a company that provides merchants with the ability to accept online payments without requiring a merchant account

3) a form of currency that is available only in digital or electronic form, and not in physical form. It is also called digital money, electronic money, electronic currency, or cyber cash.

4) a completed agreement between a buyer and a seller to exchange goods, services, or financial assets which happened in store and face-to-face

5) a type of two-dimensional bar code that consists of square black modules on a white background which is designed to be read by smartphones

6) selling related or complementary products to an existing customer

7) a secure method for consumers to purchase products or services using a debit, credit, smartcard, or another payment device by using radio frequency identification (RFID) technology and near-field communication (NFC)

( ) A. quick response code

( ) B. third-party payment company

( ) C. in-store transaction

( ) D. cross-selling

( ) E. logistics system

( ) F. digital currency

( ) G. contactless payment

Pretask

You are currently an intern of Alibaba and your team leader would like to promote and popularize the Alipay in India. You have been assigned to design a poster to illustrate the characteristics of digital payments in China and introduce Alipay and predict its prospect in India.

1) To accomplish the task, I plan to take the following steps:

_____.

For the first step, I think _____

might be challenging.

For the second step, I think _____

might be challenging.

_____

_____

2) I expect to achieve the following goals after learning the unit:

_____

_____

Passage

China: A Digital Payments Revolution

This article is an excerpt from https://www.cgap.org/research/publication/china-digital-payments-revolution (September, 2019). The author probes into the digital payments in China and goes behind the phenomenon which influences the world with two giant mobile payments products Alipay and WeChat Pay. This article goes deep into how these two mobile payments products leverage the advantages of digital payments in China to launch this great revolution and also analyzes how they drive the wallet use by adopting different approaches.

pioneer /ˌpaɪəˈnɪə(r)/
v. to be one of the first people to do, discover, or use sth. new

shift /ʃɪft/
n. a change in position or direction

account for
to be a particular amount or part of something

transaction /trænˈzækʃn/
n. a piece of business that is done between people, especially an act of buying or selling

1   Chinese giants Alibaba and Tencent **pioneered** digital merchant payments and have driven the **shift** away from cash in the Chinese economy, where they now **account for** 90 percent of the $17 trillion mobile payments market. This rapid shift was enabled by the country's widespread bank account and smartphone ownership, but nevertheless holds clear lessons for providers in less advanced markets.

The Market: Firms and Products

2   China's estimated 527 million unique mobile payment users made **transactions** totaling around $17 trillion in 2017—more than double the 2016 figure. (See Figure 3–1) The number of people making mobile merchant payments is expected to rise to 577 million in 2019 and to almost 700

million in 2022. Digital payments are becoming so dominant that the People's Bank of China[1] has had to forbid what it sees as **discrimination** against cash by merchants who accept only digital payments. This is all the more **remarkable** because just two decades ago, China was **basically** a cash economy.

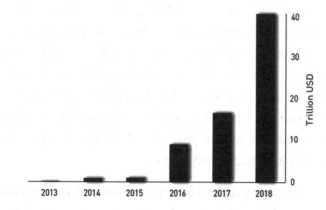

Figure 3–1   Total value of mobile payments in China

Source: FT[2]

3   In many regards, this success is thanks to two Chinese tech **juggernauts** whose brands now **reverberate** around the world: the e-commerce giant Alibaba and the gaming company Tencent, with its social media platform WeChat.

4   These two mobile payments products have rapidly reshaped China's payments landscape. With monthly active users of over 500 million (Alipay) and 900 million (WeChat Pay), they have created a massively valuable mobile payments market that they completely dominate (93 percent of the mobile

---

1 People's Bank of China was established on Dec. 1, 1948, and is responsible for monetary policy and fiscal regulation in China. It is one of the largest central banks in the world, with over $3 trillion in foreign exchange reserves.

2 FT refers to *Financial Times*, which is one of the world's leading news organizations, recognized internationally for its authority, integrity, and accuracy.

discrimination
/dɪˌskrɪmɪˈneɪʃn/
n. the practice of treating sb. or a particular group in society less fairly than others

remarkable
/rɪˈmɑːkəbl/
adj. unusual or surprising in a way that causes people to take notice

basically /ˈbeɪsɪkli/
adv. in the most important ways, without considering things that are less important

juggernaut
/ˈdʒʌɡənɔːt/
n. a large and powerful force or institution that cannot be controlled

reverberate
/rɪˈvɜːbəreɪt/
v. to be repeated several times as it is reflected off different surfaces

payment segment is controlled by the two). More than 20 million users make purchases every day through WeChat Pay, and 200,000 people sign up for the service every day.

5 Much of this growth has taken place on the back of quick response (QR) codes, which were invented in Japan in 1994 but never really gained **traction** until taking off in China. WeChat Pay and Alipay introduced **proprietary** versions of QR codes in 2011 and, by 2016, more than $1.65 trillion in transactions used the codes. Recent numbers suggest that the vast majority of the $5.5 trillion mobile payments made in a year were handled via QR code on WeChat and Alipay apps.

6 Both companies have since leveraged the massive uptake of their app-based online payments products to successfully move into merchant payments. Around one-third of consumer payments in China are now cashless, and three-fourths of Chinese smartphone users made a mobile point-of-sale purchase in 2017 (compared with one-fourth of American users). This is almost exclusively thanks to Alipay and WeChat Pay. How did they do it? Let's get into the details.

Merchant Payments in China: Key Features

7 Two key enabling factors in China made it **ripe** for a digital payments and retail revolution. The first is high levels of bank account ownership (79 percent), which served as a foundation for funding the mobile wallets. Alipay and WeChat Pay were able to **ride on** existing financial infrastructure in the form of bank accounts and bank cards and clearing and settlement systems. In fact, both companies are classified as "third-party payment companies", which highlights their reliance on an **underlying** bank account. The

---

traction /'trækʃn/
n. the extent to which an idea, a product, etc. becomes popular or gain support

proprietary /prə'praɪətri/
adj. made and sold by a particular company and protected by a registered trademark

ripe /raɪp/
adj. ready or suitable for sth. to happen

ride on to depend on sth.

underlying /ˌʌndə'laɪŋ/
adj. important in a situation but not always easily noticed or stated clearly

second is widespread smartphone ownership, which rose from 29 percent in 2013 to 71 percent in 2016 (Findex[3], 2014). Smartphones combined with bank accounts allowed users to easily link their accounts to their phones through an app.

8   In this environment, Alipay and WeChat made smart choices to drive wallet use. Most importantly, they created a strong customer-value **proposition** by deploying payments not as an end in itself, but as a gateway to a vast digital ecosystem of products and services. Alipay and WeChat Pay both link users' wallets directly to in-app retail platforms that also include financial services, such as investment and insurance products, e-commerce services, and convenient solutions for bill pay. Their apps link users' bank cards to a smartphone application, which **in turn** enables an endless list of offline and online consumption and bill payment services—from taxi hailing and grocery delivery to utilities and credit card payments, to booking wedding venues and investing in financial products. More than 1 million restaurants, 40,000 supermarkets and convenience stores, 1 million taxis, and 300 hospitals are connected to the Alipay app.

9   Among many other benefits of this approach, **seamlessly** integrating ordering and payment helps avoid having to compete with cash. Whereas for an

proposition
/ˌprɒpəˈzɪʃn/
n. an idea or a plan of action that is suggested, especially in business

in turn
    as a result of sth. in a series of events

seamlessly /ˈsiːmləsli/
adv. smoothly, so that you do not notice any change between one part and the next

---

3 Findex refers to the Global Findex database, which is the world's most comprehensive data set on how adults save, borrow, make payments, and manage risk. Launched with funding from the Bill & Melinda Gates Foundation, the database has been published every three years since 2011. The data are collected in partnership with Gallup, Inc., through nationally representative surveys of more than 150,000 adults in over 140 economies. And it adds new data on the use of financial technology (fintech), including the use of mobile phones and the Internet to conduct financial transactions.

self-evident
/ˌself ˈevɪdənt/
adj. so obvious that there is no need for proof or explanation

minimal /ˈmɪnɪml/
adj. very small in size or amount; as small as possible

threshold /ˈθreʃhəʊld/
n. the level at which sth. starts to happen or have an effect
refund /rɪˈfʌnd/
v. to give people their money back, especially because they have paid too much or because they are not satisfied with sth. they bought

in-store transaction like buying a pizza, the choice between cash and mobile payments is not **self-evident**; when ordering through this new approach, the payment is already made by the time the pizza is delivered. While cash on delivery is theoretically also possible, it is a clunky option.

10　To drive uptake, the companies have also created easy on-boarding for customers and merchants. Customers self-enroll through the app, and sellers can start accepting digital payments by sharing their individual QR code even before registering as merchants. This first step lowers the bar for testing digital payments in the business and has helped many make the transition. Initial documentation requirements are **minimal**: New customers must link their payments wallet to an existing bank card or account, allowing mobile payments providers to leverage existing customer due diligence (CDD)[4] information for that bank account. As merchants' volumes increase, providers typically ask for additional information to deepen their CDD.

11　To encourage wide uptake and drive volume, both companies take a relatively light approach to transaction fees, so as not to create the type of pricing or behavioral barriers that can otherwise be a significant challenge. If the merchant's monthly transaction volume is lower than a certain **threshold**, Alipay and WeChat Pay **refund** the commission, whereas merchants transacting above the threshold pay between 0.6 percent and 1 percent of the

---

4　Customer due diligence, or CDD, is the process where relevant information about the customer is collected and evaluated for any potential risk for the organization or money laundering or terrorist financing activities. CDD is essential for KYC (Know Your Client), and although these processes differ around the globe, they have a single aim—to identify your customers and their activities.

transaction value. This ensures that small businesses can use the service virtually for free, while it also creates fee revenue from companies who use the service a lot. Like person-to-person payments, merchant payments are free of charge for end customers, though customers must pay a 0.1 percent fee when they withdraw amounts above a threshold ($153 for WeChat and $2,897 for Alipay) from their e-wallets. This fee structure is designed less to generate revenue than to encourage users to leave funds in the wallet and spend them within the ecosystem.

12   Part of the reason that the Chinese mobile payments giants keep transaction fees relatively low is that they recognize the cross-selling opportunity that comes from other parts of their digital ecosystem. As customers start using their digital wallets as their payments instrument of choice for day-to-day purchases, they also become much more likely to buy any of the **myriad** other products and services **embedded** in the wallet. About 640 million people use more than one category of product in this ecosystem, and 190 million use five or more. These opportunities for cross-selling can be significant. For example, Alibaba's Yu'e Bao grew to become the largest money market fund in the world in just four years, with $233 billion under management, representing 25 percent of China's money market industry.

13   Another reason Alibaba and WeChat keep fees low is that both recognize the value of the data they get access to and the insights these generate on the preferences of both individual customers and specific segments. These insights can be used to refine sales and marketing of existing products and to spur the creation of entirely new ones, including merchant

myriad
/ˈmɪriəd/
adj. extremely large in number
embed /ɪmˈbed/
v. to fix sth. firmly into a substance or solid object

underwrite /ˌʌndəˈraɪt/
v. to accept financial responsibility for an activity so that you will pay money in case loss or damage happens

accelerator
/əkˈseləreɪtə(r)/
n. the pedal in a car or other vehicle that you press with your foot to control the speed of the engine

credit and other financial services **underwritten** on the basis of the payments and other data collected through the ecosystem. These types of VAS[5] can be powerful **accelerators** of digital payments by attracting merchants to the platform and generating revenue outside of transaction fees.

14 The data generated can also be used in other ways. Notably, they are a central enabler of the fundamental transformation of retail commerce that Alibaba founder Jack Ma has labeled "New Retail"[6]. This shift to New Retail relies on data to not only power ever better services to merchants, but to reinvent the logistics systems delivering goods to both merchants and end consumers and to create product development processes that are far faster, more interactive, and tailored to customer preferences than traditional methods.

15 Both companies have also taken a savvy approach to driving consumer excitement. In 2014, WeChat Pay famously created a digital version of the traditional "red envelope" gift exchange to drive acceptance of the payments mechanism. This became an instant

5 VAS refers to value added services, which are non-core services or features that are beyond the standard voice calls. This term is very popular in the telecommunications industry though it can be used in almost any service industry in reference to services that are availed at no or at a little cost to promote the primary business. Core services are mainly basic services, support services, and complementary services. Conceptually, telecommunications companies use value added services to improve the value of their standard service offerings and to spur subscribers to use their primary services more and drive up the average revenue per user.

6 New Retail is a term coined by Jack Ma, the founder of Alibaba, in 2016 to describe how offline, online, and logistics businesses were merging to create an integrated retail sector that would seamlessly blend what were previously separate spaces. Describing it as one of five areas that will be fundamentally transformed by innovation— the others being finance, manufacturing, technology, and energy— Ma asserted that New Retail should be the key strategic priority for e-commerce and payments businesses.

hit with consumers and contributed to the service's rapid growth. Similar products are now available from all of China's major payments platforms.

16   Another customer **incentive** is loyalty rewards, to which Alipay executives give significant credit for driving uptake and volumes. This year, Alipay is offering **subsidies** totaling 500 million yuan ($73.6 million) for a *hongbao* (red envelope) campaign to reward customer loyalty[7]. A few years ago, a similar campaign featured incentives such as bus rides, **rebates**, and even gold. In 2017, Alipay set aside 1 billion yuan ($160 million) in cash-back incentives for purchases made through Alipay to get shoppers to use the service more often. While Alibaba and Tencent initially offered generous incentives to get merchants to go digital, ultimately, rapidly changing customer preferences drove uptake.

17   Finally, the choice of QR codes as the main acceptance technology has enabled rapid **scaling up** and widespread acceptance of digital payments. QR codes have many advantages—they are cheap and easy for both customers and merchants to adopt. Alipay and WeChat Pay tested various technologies, including near-field communication[8], before **opting** to use QR (static as well as dynamic). Furthermore,

incentive /ɪnˈsentɪv/
n. sth. that encourages you to work harder, start a new activity, etc.
subsidy /ˈsʌbsədi/
n. money that is paid by a government or an organization to reduce the costs of services or of producing goods so that their prices can be kept low
rebate /ˈriːbeɪt/
n. an amount of money that is taken away from the cost of sth., before you pay for it

scale up
to increase the size or number of sth.

opt /ɒpt/
v. to choose to take or not to take a particular course of action

---

7 Loyalty reward refers to a program which gives repeat shoppers added benefits and promotions. Each purchase earns some sort of reward. Reward programs are great for customer retention and loyalty because they encourage repeat purchases. Loyalty reward may be referral- or purchase-based (or both). It may be cash back, points-based, referral-based, tiered, and paid. You can run your loyalty reward program online or with a tangible item like a punch card.

8 Near-field communication or NFC, is a short-range wireless technology that makes your smartphone, tablet, wearables, payment cards, and other devices even smarter. Near-field communication is the ultimate in connectivity. With NFC, you can transfer information between devices quickly and easily with a single touch—whether paying bills, exchanging business cards, downloading coupons, or sharing a research paper.

interoperable
/ˌɪntərˈɒpərəbl/
adj. of or relating
to the ability
to share data
between different
computer systems

the People's Bank of China announced it intended to regulate QR codes to improve security, and it is creating an online settlement platform, called Wanglian, for nonbank institutions. These moves, combined with a global trend toward standardized QR codes, suggest that mobile payments may soon be **interoperable** in China.

(1,715 words)

Theme-Related Words & Expressions

mobile payment	移动支付
cash economy	现金经济
sign up for	注册；登记报名
quick response code	二维码
uptake	客户率
point-of-sale	销售点
bank account ownership	银行账户所有权
clearing and settlement system	清算及结算系统
third-party payment company	第三方支付公司
customer-value proposition	客户价值主张
investment and insurance product	投资及保险产品
e-commerce service	电子商务服务
bill pay	支付账单
taxi hailing	打车
grocery delivery	送货
book wedding venues	预定婚礼场地
invest in financial products	投资金融产品
in-store transaction	店内支付交易

on-boarding	入职；登录
self-enroll	用户自己登录
customer due diligence (CDD)	客户尽职调查
commission	佣金
person-to-person payments	面对面付款
end customer	终端客户
cross-selling	交叉销售
VAS (value added service)	增值服务
New Retail	新零售
logistics system	物流系统
customer preference	客户喜好
customer excitement	客户热情
customer incentive	客户激励措施
loyalty reward	忠诚度奖励
near-field communication (NFC)	近场通信；近距离无线通信技术

Prepare/Probe

❶ Reading Comprehension

Answer the following questions according to the passage.

1) How did the Alipay and WeChat Pay reshape China's payments landscape?

_____

_____

2) Which two factors in China made it ripe for a digital payments and retail revolution?

_____

_____

3) How do you understand "New Retail"?

_____

_____

4) How did Alibaba and Tencent drive consumer excitement?

_____

_____

5) How did the digital payments influence the real life?

_____

_____

Ⅱ Structure Building

Check your understanding of the overall structure of the passage by completing the following diagram.

The Digital Payments Market in China	
In many regards, this success on digital payments in China is thanks to two Chinese tech companies: Alibaba and Tencent. (Paras. 2–6)	• This success is owed to two Chinese tech companies who 1) _____ around the world. • Those two companies 2) _____ a massively valuable mobile payments market in China. • The growth of the payments market 3) _____ on the back of quick response (QR) codes.
The Key Features of Merchant Payments in China	
The features of China's merchants payment and other feasible approaches two companies adopted. (Paras. 7–17)	• Two key 4) _____ factors in China made it ripe for a digital payments and revolution. • The first is high levels of bank account ownership, and the second is 5) _____ smartphone ownership.

Practice

❶ Vocabulary Practice

1. Match the following theme-related words and expressions in Column A with their Chinese equivalents in Column B.

Column A	Column B
1) loyalty reward	A. 激发消费者热情
2) New Retail	B. 第三方支付公司
3) sign up for	C. 影响巨大；产生回响
4) cash economy	D. 忠诚度奖励
5) tailor customer preferences	E. 现金经济
6) self-enroll	F. 对银行账户的依赖
7) third-party payment company	G. 注册；登记报名
8) customer incentive	H. 新零售
9) reverberate	I. 物流系统
10) reliance on bank account	J. 用户自己登录
11) logistics system	K. 满足客户的喜好
12) drive customer excitement	L. 客户激励措施

2. Fill in the blanks with the words or phrases in the box. Change the form if necessary.

give credit to	get access to	hit	enabling	reverberate
leverage	take off	spur	scale up	option

1) WeChat Pay and Alipay have totally changed the landscape of payments in China, whose effect _____ throughout the whole way of merchant.

2) The quick response codes did not gain any attraction in the world until _____ in China.

3) Those third-party payment companies _____ the high levels of bank account ownership to promote the mobile wallets.

4) Chinese widespread smartphone ownership provides a(n) _____ environment for the digital payments and retail revolution.

5) WeChat recognized the value of data they _____ and based on which they acquired the customer preferences.

6) The success of Chinese digital payments could _____ the two Chinese tech companies.

7) Ant Forest turns Alipay users' environmentally friendly actions into "green energy", which they can use to plant and nurture a real tree. Hence, digital payments can _____ green living in a way.

8) The green energy feeds the virtual trees of Ant Forest. When the user's tree is big enough in the virtual world, they have a(n) _____ to have the Alipay plant a real tree or adopt a patch of protected land.

9) Alipay's Ant Forest turns green choices into trees. It is a viable model for _____ public climate action.

10) WeChat Pay created a digital version of "red envelop", which became an instant _____ with customers and is still running on during the Spring Festival.

Ⅱ Sentence Practice

1. **Study the sentence structure first, and then translate each of the given Chinese sentences into English by imitating the sentence structure.**

1) In many regards, this success is <u>thanks to</u> two Chinese tech juggernauts whose brands now reverberate around the world: the e-commerce giant Alibaba and the gaming company Tencent, with its social media platform WeChat. (Para. 3)

翻译：得益于国防科技和武器装备重大工程的实施，我国科技加速向战斗力转化。

_____

_____

2) Much of this growth has taken place on the back of quick response (QR) codes, which were invented in Japan in 1994 but never really gained traction <u>until</u> taking off in China. (Para.5)

翻译：我们要坚持目标导向、行动导向，咬定青山不放松，一张蓝图绘到底。

_____

_____

3) To encourage wide uptake and drive volume, both companies take a relatively light approach to transaction fees, <u>so as not to</u> create the type

of pricing or behavioral barriers that can otherwise be a significant challenge. (Para.11)

翻译：全心全意依靠工人阶级，健全以职工代表大会为基本形式的企事业单位民主管理制度，以保证职工合法权益不受侵犯。

_____

_____

4) This fee structure <u>is</u> designed <u>less</u> to generate revenue <u>than</u> to encourage users to leave funds in the wallet and spend them within the ecosystem. (Para.11)

翻译：坚持以马克思主义为指导，不是背诵和重复其具体结论和词句，而是要运用其科学的世界观和方法论解决中国的问题。

_____

_____

5) Another customer incentive is loyalty rewards, <u>to</u> which Alipay executives <u>give significant credit</u> for driving uptake and volumes. (Para.16)

翻译：全社会研发经费增长是中国能够进入创新型国家行列的重要原因。

_____

_____

Ⅲ Discourse Practice

1. **Sequence the following disordered paragraphs into a whole to form a passage which is about the history and origin of digital payments. In the process, you'd better pay attention to the transitional devices and the logic of the passage.**

A. Payments are made by using payment instruments. Check and cash are examples of payment instruments. However, digital payment is not a single instrument but rather an umbrella term that is applied to many instruments used in various ways. It can be defined as a way of paying for services or goods via an electronic medium without the use of cash or check. It is also known as electronic payment system or e-payment.

B. Due to the wide spread of Internet-based shopping and banking, digital payment system grew fast. With technology development, many digital payments companies have been established to increase, improve and offer secure e-payment transactions.

C. Along with the development of the Internet, online payments began to operate in the 1990s. Established in 1994, Stanford Federal Credit Union was the first institution to offer online banking services to all its customers. Initially, online payment systems were not user-friendly and needed specialized knowledge of data transfer protocol.

D. Finally, after realizing that its customers preferred PayPal as their payment solution, eBay acquired PayPal. After some years, PayPal realized it was spending a lot of resources to improve the shopping experience on eBay instead of focusing on reducing friction for customers of the payments market. In September 2014, three weeks after Apple launched Apple Pay, eBay announced PayPal's separation. Meanwhile, Alipay quietly surpassed PayPal and became the biggest mobile payment solution with approximately $150 billion worth of transactions in 2013.

E. In 1998, PayPal began as a mobile payment firm with wireless transactions on Palm Pilots. However, it later focused on online payment when it established a strong customer base on eBay, a company that had a powerful auction platform. PayPal continued to create innovations one after another like sending payments using email addresses, launching the reverse Turing test to reduce fraud and making HTML payment buttons.

F. In the beginning, the major players in the digital payment market were Millicent and Ecash, founded in 1995 and 1996 respectively. Most of the first online services used micropayment systems and their shared characteristic was the attempt to have electronic cash alternatives (like e-money, tokens or digital cash). Moreover, the Amazon (one of the e-commerce pioneers) was founded in 1994.

G. The origin of digital payment is associated with the beginning of the Internet, which changed the world as nothing before. If there was no Internet, there wouldn't be e-services and online stores. The Internet history began in 1969 with ARPANET, the military network that was meant to be communication network during the Vietnam War period. However, the main turning point occurred in 1989 when Tim Berners-Lee discovered the so-called "pages" or "sites" that made it easier to access and publish information on the Internet.

H. Not only did eBay try to defeat PayPal with monopolistic power and marketing gimmicks but also financial institutions such as banks attempted to pursue legal means against the company to categorize it as an unsecured service or a bank.

I. When eBay sellers started to enlist in PayPal, eBay felt threatened. It responded by creating Billpoint that mimicked much core functionality of PayPal. Instead of building innovative features to reduce friction for customers, the company began to cajole users into accepting Billpoint by exercising more control over its platform. Some tactics used by eBay included offering free listing days to Billpoint users, requiring the use of Billpoint for its Stores sites and cutting fees.

Sequence: _____

Produce

Make an Eye-Catching Poster

❶ Recap of the Previous Sessions

In Pretest, you've gained a basic understanding of digital payments in China. In Prepare/Probe, you've grasped the main idea and structure of the text. In Practice, you've familiarized yourself with the necessary language points, sentence patterns, and the key information needed for Produce. Now, it's time to consider the production of an eye-catching poster.

❷ Definition of a Poster

Poster is usually a large printed sheet that often contains pictures and is posted in a public place (so as to promote something). Posters are one of the oldest, most tried and true types of marketing collateral. Posters are also an effective way to draw attention to your sales, products, events, fundraisers and more.

Ⅲ Steps of Making a Poster

1. Identify the goal of your poster

The goal of designing a poster is either to create social awareness about issues related to current problems and needs, or to advertise or even to extend public invitations and display notices. The goal of your poster decides the whole effect. For example, if you want to inform the relative information of a conference, the poster design should emphasize the key information attendees will need to know. If the poster informs qualified candidates about the open position, the open position and other relevant information should be highlighted.

If the poster aims to illustrate the summary of a research to present the scientific discoveries to larger audiences, scientific poster is necessary to be made. The scientific poster is always organized, clean, simple design. It focuses on one specific research topic that can be explained in 5–15 minutes. The scientific poster contains Title, Authors, Abstract, Introduction, Materials & Methods, Results, Discussion, References and Acknowledgments. It has four to ten high-resolution figures and/or tables that describe the research in detail and contains minimal text, with figures and tables being the main focus.

The poster can also be used as the product promotion, software announcement, activity forecasting, movie introduction, research publicizing or exhibition advertising. Its purpose is to inform and persuade, to attract attention and generate discussion. So it should be clear and understandable to the audience. The design and content of the poster should be considered in the perspective of its ultimate purpose.

2. Consider your target audience

Effective communication starts with knowing your audience. For whom are you designing this poster and what do they want to see? Put yourself in the shoes of your target audience before getting started on your design. Think carefully about the language you use and the assumption you make about your viewer's knowledge. If the poster aims to attract attention from the professional area, the formal layout, colors and design are needed. On the contrary, if the poster is supposed to appeal to younger group of people, it should be decorated with vivid color and bold fonts.

3. Decide your titles

Titles are usually the neglected step-child of the poster. Most of us have gone through years of schooling with admonitions from various teachers to put a title on our papers, but few of us have been given much—if any—instruction on how to write a title, what its function is, or why it is important. In fact, unless they are given a template specifying where and how to set the title, some writers format it the same as the rest of the paper. But in an age where readers are always in a hurry and want to get as much as possible out of their reading with the least possible effort, titles take on the extremely important roles of bringing your readers to the paper, especially to a poster and, once there, engaging them in its content. If the readers have a choice of a dozen or more papers to read, they will start with the ones that seem to best meet their needs for understanding a concept or solving a problem. A title that captures the content of the paper and communicates it to the readers increases the chance that the paper will be read. How to draft the title? Here are ten tips for adding a great title for your poster.

- Choose a title that is relevant to your theme but also shows your creativity. A creative title such as "It's Electric" for an Electricity-themed science fair project is both relevant and witty enough to get your poster noticed.

- Try to state your main point in a single sentence or with as few words as possible. A title that is too long will cause problems for both the layout of your poster board as well as the readability.

- Keep your title vibrant and legible from at least 4 feet away. Science fair and contest judges, as well as regular viewers must be able to read your poster in order to understand it. Bold lettering in one solid color is always a safe bet and assures that your title is legible from far away.

- Write your title on an angle to give the illusion of movement. This technique would be great when you make a poster about skiing or snowboarding.

- You don't have to put your title all in one place. Consider positioning segments of your poster title in different locations to give your poster a dramatic effect. This will make your poster stand out from the rest as well as draw attention to different areas of your poster board.

- A border around your title can emphasize your poster's theme. You can choose a simple border such as a colored box or use images to frame your title and add to the theme. For example, use clip art images of lemons to frame your title for a lemonade stand poster.

- Instead of using bullet points, accent your poster titles and headings with small symbols or pictures that reinforce your theme. The easiest way to do this is by using Sparkle Poster Stickers.

- Arching your title over a large image is an artistic way to get your audience's attention.

- Slightly jumbled letters in bold colors are perfect for a fun or playful title. Just tilt each letter in the opposite direction from the previous letter and you have a fun new look.

- Enclose your title in a memorable shape to give instant spark to your poster. A great way to do this is by using small pre-cut poster board shapes as a background.

Now you can try the following exercise.

Which title is informative and simple, and suitable for each poster? Then state your reasons.

For the book promotion poster: *Heart of Darkness*   Yes ( ) No ( )

_____

_____

For the science fair poster: Science Fair 2015: Alcohol and Teens

Yes ( ) No ( )

_____

_____

For the product promotion poster: Biggest Sales! Shop Now!

Yes ( ) No ( )

_____

_____

For the activity forecasting poster: Pride Color Run   Yes ( ) No ( )

_____

_____

For the movie advertising poster: Come and see, the *Interstella* would be released on 15 this month.   Yes ( ) No ( )

---

4. Describe the product/event/conference details

What details you choose to include on your poster will depend on the function of your poster. You have to make it easy to read from a distance and inform the details—What, when, and where. Answer these questions in the second level of the text (The title or the headline is the first level of the text). What information do people need to do what your poster is asking of them? Provide the information here in a concise manner to let them acquire the maximal and the most complete information in the quickest glance. As for sizing, there are two options—drop the size to about half of the main headline for very clear hierarchy or continue to use a larger size and use another technique for contrast (The choice often depends on other elements and the importance of the secondary text).

5. Choose the proper graphics, colors and fonts of the poster to make it a visual hierarchy of information

For example, if you are creating an event poster, the information on your poster should be read in this order: the name of your event; the date and time of your event; a short description of the event or a catchy tagline; the location of your event (if you choose to include it); a simple call-to-action like a website, social media page or contact number; the name of your company, department, organization, etc. So do the graphics, colors and fonts. The production of an eye-catching poster needs the striking contrast in a short glance.

After you finish the steps above, you may open your computer and make an eye-catching poster on Chinese digital payments (see details in Pre-task). You can use the outline below to help you.

➢ Your title: _____.

➢ The words to inform the detail of the product: _____

_____.

➢ Other elements you should list in your poster: _____.

➢ The graphics, color and fonts you will apply in your poster:

_____

_____

Post-Learning Evaluation

No.	Statements	Strongly agree	Agree	Not sure	Disagree	Strongly disagree
1	I have grasped the expressions related to the theme.					
2	I am familiar with the key words and phrases in the passage.					
3	I am familiar with the major points of the passage.					
4	I am familiar with the terms explained in the footnotes.					
5	I have grasped the steps of making an eye-catching poster.					
6	I have a better understanding of China's great revolution about digital payments.					
7	I take pride in China's rapid advances in techniques and developments about digital payments.					
8	I would form a more critical view towards the Western coverage on digital payments, and if there are some misunderstandings, I would like to explain.					
9	I understand my role in the accomplishment of the project, and I have improved my teamwork skills by collaborating with my team members.					
10	I am proud of China's contribution to digital payments.					
11	After learning this chapter, I will tell the story on Chinese digital payments to international friends when I have the opportunity.					

Chapter 4

China's Online Education

Pretest

How much do you know about China's online education? Can you match the service modes of online education with their correct descriptions? You may go to our MOOC (4.3 Online Education) to learn more before taking this quiz.

1) being comprised of four modules—education resources database, online classes, exam system, and discussion groups

2) varying in terms of forms; there are tools for memorizing words, taking notes, question banks, early childhood education, as well as tools for testing and consulting

3) aiming at improving and elevating education quality

4) mainly including traditional online schools and distance schools

(　　) A. tool providers

(　　) B. technical equipment providers

(　　) C. course content producers

(　　) D. platform resources aggregators

Pretask

You and two of your classmates are invited to an international online forum on online education. The forum will bring together students from various countries, and each team of participants is required to talk about the latest developments in online education within their own country. Your team decide to explore how COVID-19 has shaped China's online education, and have searched an article for reference. Within your team, you are responsible for designing PowerPoint slides and organizing their presentation.

1) To accomplish the task, I plan to take the following steps:

_____ .

For the first step, I think _____
might be challenging.
For the second step, I think _____
might be challenging.

_____

_____

2) I expect to achieve the following goals after learning the unit:

_____

_____

Passage
The Impact of COVID-19 on China's Education

This article is adapted from a report developed by Oliver Wyman, a leading international management consulting firm (March, 2020). It summarizes the implications of COVID-19 on China's education industry by exploring the industry's different subsectors, the potential changes to customer behavior and key market trends.

tertiary /ˈtɜːʃəri/
adj. third in order, rank or importance
adversely /ˈædvɜːsli/
adv. in a negative and unpleasant manner

1   China's education industry is an important component of its **tertiary** sector. The industry has been **adversely** affected by the COVID-19 outbreak, arousing extensive societal attention and discussion. Complaints during this period have primarily been about the poor quality of some online classes, the low ratings gained by some learning apps, the cancellation of major exams, and the stress over searching for and finding suitable jobs. Given the outbreak's tremendous and profound impact on the market's landscape and dynamics, Oliver Wyman here summarizes the implications to the industry's different sub-segments and the potential changes to customer behavior, so as to highlight key market trends and **identify** segmental opportunities during this critical time.

identify /aɪˈdentɪfaɪ/
v. to find or discover sb./sth.

China's Education Industry Segmentation

2   The segmentation is based on the core nature of the different sub-sectors. The education industry

here refers to the private segment only. The public segment is not covered. We estimate that China's education industry will witness negative growth in 2020. While school businesses will remain stable due to **resilient** demand, training businesses will suffer a serious economic **blow**, with the exception of a few sub-segments, such as businesses that focus on test preparation for admission into higher-learning institutes. Separately, the adoption of online education will accelerate, but the respective increase in terms of the number of paid users will still be limited. Meanwhile, online competition will be home to the Matthew Effect[1], while the gap between the leading and lagging offline players will widen, and many medium-to-small-sized training businesses will be eliminated due to a lack of cash flow[2]. Consolidation will take place in the experience-based education segment, where demand has **shrunk** drastically due to the heavy reliance on commuting to various teaching venues. The big winners are players that focus on providing offerings to businesses, as the demand for these offerings has grown **exponentially** since the beginning of the outbreak.

resilient /rɪˈzɪliənt/
adj. able to recover quickly after sth. unpleasant such as shock, injury, etc.

blow /bləʊ/
n. a sudden event which has damaging effects on sb./sth.

shrink /ʃrɪŋk/
v. to become or to make sth. smaller in size or amount

exponentially /ˌekspəˈnenʃəli/
adv. in an exponential manner

Five Political, Economic and Macro-Environmental Influences

3   Institutions, from kindergartens up to universities,

---

1 Matthew Effect is a social phenomenon often linked to the idea that the rich get richer and the poor get poorer. In essence, this refers to a common concept that those who already have status are often placed in situations where they gain more, and those that do not have status typically struggle to achieve more.

2 Cash flow is the net amount of cash and cash-equivalents being transferred into and out of a business. At the most fundamental level, a company's ability to create value for shareholders is determined by its ability to generate positive cash flows.

recommencement
/ˌriːkə'mensmənt/
n. beginning again

make up for
to do or have sth. as a way of correcting or improving sth. else

call for
to publicly ask for sth. to happen
suspension /sə'spenʃn/
n. the act of delaying or stopping sth. for a while, until a decision is made

squeeze /skwiːz/
v. to press sth. firmly
supervision
/ˌsuːpə'vɪʒən/
n. management by overseeing the performance or operation of a person or group
postpone /pə'spəʊn/
v. to arrange for an event, etc. to take place at a later time or date

are required to delay the **recommencement** of the spring semester. The Ministry of Education has launched an initiative to "ensure learning is undisrupted when classes are disrupted" to encourage all schools to leverage online platforms to continue teaching. In order to **make up for** lost time after traditional class is resumed, schools in some provinces such as Shandong and Guangdong, will either adopt a six-school-day a week schedule or shorten the summer break.

4　The Ministry of Education has **called for** the **suspension** of all offline training programs and gatherings by training providers. According to the notice issued by the Ministry of Education, training providers cannot restart their offline operations until schools officially reopen, so most of them will need to wait until May. Moreover, with schools needing to make up for lost time, these providers' course hours are likely to be further **squeezed**. Additionally, online training is under strict **supervision**. Any violation, such as super-syllabus teaching, test-oriented teaching, false advertising, or exam ranking, will be investigated and punished accordingly.

5　Entrance examinations and standardized tests have been **postponed** or cancelled. The Ministry of Education has postponed the following: self-taught higher education examinations, the registration of graduate admission tests for candidates of equivalent learning capabilities, and primary and secondary school teacher qualification and teacher certification examinations. New schedules will be announced at a later date. Meanwhile, some standardized tests, such as the SAT, GMAT, GRE, TOEFL, and IELTS, have been cancelled in February and March. Students also cannot sit for these tests in other regions due to the current travel bans in place.

6 Customers' willingness to pay may be lower if economic growth further slows. According to Oliver Wyman, China's gross domestic product (GDP) growth may still range from 5.8% to 6% in 2020 with strong government stimulus. Without government intervention though, it could **slump** to between 5% and 5.5%. Slowing economic growth and decreasing disposable income during the COVID-19 outbreak may weaken customers' affordability with regard to spending on education. On the other hand, the government is taking measures to help **offset** the weakening demand in the job market, such as creating more job opportunities by creating more entry-level positions in the public sector and encouraging students to join the army. It is also offering more tertiary-education seats, with 190,000 more seats in master and doctorate programs, and 320,000 more seats in bachelor programs.

slump /slʌmp/
v. to fall in price, value, number, etc., suddenly and by a large amount

offset /ˈɒfset/
v. to use one cost, payment or situation in order to cancel or reduce the effect of another

7 The situation caused by the outbreak remains **grim**. Since late February, the surge in COVID-19 cases in some countries and regions has deepened the complexity and uncertainty of the economy in the short term. A number of international flights have been cancelled, and visas for several countries and regions have been suspended.

grim /grɪm/
adj. unpleasant and depressing

8 In light of the above, Oliver Wyman expects the following in terms of customer behavior:

- Affordability will be **suppressed**. Parents will be more prudent about spending on supplementary education for their children. Moreover, as price **sensitivity** will increase, spending on premium education offerings may be impacted.
- Fewer students will pursue short-term study abroad programs. The cancellation of standardized tests, travel bans, and the general

suppress /səˈpres/
v. to prevent sth. from growing, developing or continuing
sensitivity /ˌsensəˈtɪvəti/
n. responsiveness to external stimuli

end up
to find yourself in a place or situation at the end of a process or period of time

momentum
/məˈmentəm/
n. the ability to keep increasing or developing

increasing complexity of going to certain destination countries will all exert a negative impact. As such, some students may **end up** postponing or cancelling their plans to study abroad. Some short-term transnational education programs, such as outbound educational tours and summer schools, will also be postponed or cancelled.

- Growing anxiety with regard to job placement. The difficulty in finding jobs may urge students or workforce newbies to attend more training programs. As such, preparing for graduate admission tests, financial certification qualifications, and other higher-learning programs will gain **momentum** unless the outbreak impact is long term (when the prospects of finding a higher paying job are less clear).

- Increasing adoption of online education. Having online classes has been the main solution for schools and training providers amid the COVID-19 outbreak. Some online training providers have leveraged this opportunity to attract students by offering free or low-cost classes, leading to a surge in online education user numbers and adoption rates.

Key Market Segment Dynamics and Trends

9   Based on the expected changes mentioned above, we expect the dynamics and trends to take place in the following key market segments:

10   School businesses to remain stable due to resilient demand. School education is mandatory for most grade levels. The COVID-19 outbreak may change the teaching venue in the short term, but its impact

on tuition and student enrollment is **negligible**. Except for the kindergarten segment (which may see a decrease in demand by 20%), we expect to see continued resilient demand for the primary-to tertiary-level segments. In terms of cost, moving to an online teaching environment during the outbreak has increased the operational cost for a lot of schools. However, it is also a great opportunity for them to **optimize** their overall operations and transform their capabilities in terms of information technology.

11   Training businesses: strong negative impact, widening competition gap, and **irresistible** online-education trend. Training businesses consist of various sub-segments, but most have primarily adopted offline delivery models. During the COVID-19 outbreak, these offline players have tried online delivery to offset the effects of both the outbreak and its associated regulatory impacts. On the other hand, existing online players have leveraged free or low-cost classes in order to attract trial customers.

12   The market for training businesses will see negative growth this year. The three key reasons include: losses and/or refunds (of up to 20% of all business) for students who originally enrolled for the winter holiday and spring semester; course fee **discounts**, ranging from 20% to 100%, due to offline classes moving online; and the overall reduced intake of new students. As such, most providers will suffer from the spring semester to the summer break or even the fall semester, especially those that rely heavily on offline customer acquisition channels.

13   However, there are some exceptions. For example, the graduate admission test preparation segment

negligible /'neglɪdʒəbl/
adj. of very little importance or size and not worth considering

optimize /'ɒptɪmaɪz/
v. to make sth. as good as it can be; to use sth. in the best possible way

irresistible /ˌɪrɪ'zɪstəbl/
adj. so strong that sth. cannot be stopped or resisted

discount /'dɪskaʊnt/
n. an amount of money that is taken off the usual cost of sth.

may suffer from fee discounts and lower student enrollment in the first quarter of 2020, but with graduate seat numbers increasing and the labor market worsening, we expect this segment to regain momentum from the second quarter of 2020. Online training providers, such as TAL Online, Zuoyebang, and Yuanfudao, have all reported more than 20 million new users during the past six weeks. However, with a lot of customer **overlap** among competitors and low attendance rates, the quality of the trial users is relatively low. Thus, the conversion rate to full-fee paying users will likely not be as encouraging as expected. Nevertheless, online education is an irresistible trend, and customer acquisition costs should fall drastically in the short term.

14　There will be a widening competition gap between the leading and lagging offline providers during the COVID-19 outbreak. We believe the leading players with their online product capabilities and flexible long-tail operations, will survive during this period. For medium-to-small-sized offline operators that will only likely return to operation in mid-to-late May, however, we believe that over 70% of them will face a severe cash flow shortage, and nearly half of them may have to close down. The circumstances should create a great opportunity for the leading players to conduct M&As[3] and industry consolidation.

(1,518 words)

3　M&As means mergers and acquisitions. It is a general term used to describe the consolidation of companies or assets through various types of financial transactions, including mergers, acquisitions, consolidations, tender offers, purchase of assets, and management acquisitions. The term refers broadly to the process of one company combining with another.

Theme-Related Words & Expressions

tertiary sector	第三产业
low rating	低评级
industry segmentation	行业细分
experience-based education	体验式教育
super-syllabus teaching	超纲教学
test-oriented teaching	应试教学
exam ranking	考试排名
standardized test	标准化考试
self-taught higher education examinations	高等教育自学考试
candidate of equivalent learning capabilities	同等学力考生
teacher certification examination	教师资格考试
disposable income	可支配收入
outbound educational tour	出国教育旅游
workforce newbie	职场新人
graduate admission test	研究生入学考试
financial certification qualification	金融认证资格
student enrollment	招生
operational cost	运营成本
offline delivery model	线下交付模式
refund for students	给学生退费
course fee discount	课程费用打折
intake of new students	招收新学生
free or low-cost class	免费或低成本课程
customer acquisition channel	客户获取渠道
labor market	劳动力市场
attendance rate	出勤率
trial user	体验用户
conversion rate	转换率
long-tail operation	长线运营
full-fee paying user	全款付费用户
medium-to-small-sized offline operator	中小型线下运营者
M&A	并购

industry consolidation	产业整合
workers' congresses	职工代表大会
exercise strict self-governance in all respects / conduct full and rigorous Party self-governance	全面从严治党
the penetration rate of digital research and development and design tools	数字化研发设计工具普及率
internationally competitive digital industry clusters	具有国际竞争力的数字产业集群
the yardstick for education / educational evaluation	教育指挥棒
highly skilled talent	高技能人才
ICT-enabled education	教育信息化
technical and vocational education	职业技术教育
digital economy	数字经济
transformation and upgrading of traditional manufacturing industries	传统制造业转型升级
intelligent industry	智能产业
digital trade	数字贸易
promote the digitalization of education	促进教育数字化
"East Data, West Computing" project	"东数西算"工程
digital literacy and skills of the public	全民数字素养和技能
key information infrastructure	关键信息基础设施
cloud computing services	云计算服务
implement the strategy for invigorating China through science and education	实施科教兴国战略
the workforce development strategy	人才强国战略
the innovation-driven development strategy	创新驱动发展战略
self-reliance and strength in science and technology	科技自立自强
R&D spending	研发经费
leading high-tech enterprises	科技领军企业
increase investment in science and technology through diverse channels	加大多元化科技投入
master craftsmen	大国工匠
unmanned, intelligent combat capabilities	无人智能作战力量
livable, resilient, and smart cities	宜居、韧性、智慧城市

new growth drivers	新动能
the Internet of Things	物联网
informatized and intelligent warfare	信息化智能化战争

Prepare/Probe

❶ Reading Comprehension

Answer the following questions according to the passage.

1) Oliver Wyman estimates that China's education industry will witness negative growth in 2020. What's the reason for this?

_____

_____

2) Given the influences on the market, what are the potential changes to customer behavior expected by Oliver Wyman?

_____

_____

3) What are the five political, economic and macro-environmental elements that influence the development of online education in China?

_____

_____

4) Can you summarize the key market segment dynamics and trends as mentioned in the passage?

_____

_____

5) What is the severe challenge for medium-to-small-sized offline operators and what is the opportunity created for the leading players respectively?

_____

_____

Ⅲ Structure Building

Check your understanding of the overall structure of the passage by completing the following diagram.

China's Education Industry Segmentation	
It is expected that China's education industry will witness negative growth in 2020. (Para. 2)	• While school businesses will remain stable, training businesses will 1) _____. • The gap between the leading and lagging offline players will widen, and many medium-to-small-sized training businesses will be eliminated due to 2) _____. • 3) _____ will take place in the experience-based education segment.

Five Political, Economic and Macro-Environmental Influences	
Changes will be seen in the online education market due to influences from different dimensions. (Paras. 3–8)	• Institutions, from kindergartens up to universities, are required to 4) _____ the recommencement of the spring semester. • The Ministry of Education has called for the suspension of 5) _____ and gatherings by training providers. • Entrance examinations and standardized tests have been 6) _____. • Customers' willingness to pay may be 7) _____ if economic growth further slows. • The situation caused by the outbreak 8) _____.

Key Market Segment Dynamics and Trends	
The dynamics and trends will take place in some key market segments. (Paras. 9–14)	• School businesses will 9) _____ due to resilient demand. • Training businesses: strong negative impact, widening competition gap, and irresistible online-education trend. • The market for training businesses will see 10) _____ this year. • There are some exceptions, for example, the graduate admission test preparation segment.

Practice

❶ Vocabulary Practice

1. Match the following theme-related words and expressions in Column A with their Chinese equivalents in Column B.

Column A	Column B
1) 教育指挥棒	A. ICT-enabled education
2) 高技能人才	B. technical and vocational education
3) 教育信息化	C. implement the strategy for invigorating China through science and education
4) 职业技术教育	D. leading high-tech enterprises
5) 促进教育数字化	E. the yardstick for education / educational evaluation
6) 全民数字素养和技能	F. promote the digitalization of education
7) 实施科教兴国战略	G. highly skilled talent
8) 科技领军企业	H. digital literacy and skills of the public

2. Group the words and expressions related to online education. You may find the words and expressions from Exercise 1 and the reading passage. Start with the examples given below.

Tests & qualifications	*standardized test;* _____
Types of teaching and education	*experience-based education;* ____
Financial policies by online operators	*course fee discount;* _____
Types of users	*full-fee paying users;* _____
Market operation strategies by online operators	*long-tail operation;* _____

3. Fill in the blanks with the words in the box. Change the form if necessary.

slump	momentum	negligible	squeeze	discount
offset	exponential	adverse	optimize	postpone

1) Sometimes the type of policies the government makes on education _____ affects output.

2) As schools need to make up for lost time, some training providers' course hours are likely to be further _____.

3) You will receive a(n) _____ on a new Mac or iPad for your studies with Apple Education Pricing.

4) The demand for online education has grown _____ since the beginning of the COVID-19 outbreak.

5) Local administrations and enterprises should also pledge efforts to promote the construction of networks and base stations to enhance network conditions of schools, while online education platforms should continuously _____ their online services.

6) The COVID-19 outbreak may change the teaching venue in the short term, but its impact on tuition and student enrollment is _____.

7) Without government intervention though, the country's GDP could _____ to between 5% and 5.5%.

8) China's economic rebound gained _____ last month as official purchasing managers' indexes for the manufacturing and nonmanufacturing sectors both reached their highest level so far this year.

9) Critics say that virtual labs cannot _____ the loss of mentoring opportunities, especially when students are completing a thesis or dissertation.

10) Schools have decided to _____ classes due to the recent spread of the COVID-19.

Ⅱ Sentence Practice

1. **Study the sentence structure first, and then translate each of the given Chinese sentences into English by imitating the sentence structure.**

1) The industry has been adversely affected by the COVID-19 outbreak, arousing extensive societal attention and discussion. (Para. 1)

翻译：孔子学院和孔子课堂为促进多元多彩的世界文明发展作出了重要贡献，引起了世界各国的广泛关注和讨论。

_____

_____

2) The Ministry of Education has launched an initiative to encourage all schools to leverage online platforms to continue teaching. (Para. 3)

翻译：在尊重教育发展规律的基础上，政府发起了一项活动来鼓励社会力量依法兴办教育。

_____

_____

3) Some online training providers have leveraged this opportunity to attract students by offering free or low-cost classes, leading to a surge in online education user numbers and adoption rates. (Para. 8)

翻译：学生可以利用职业技术教育掌握一技之长，大幅提高家庭的可支配收入。

_____

_____

4) Based on the expected changes mentioned above, we expect the dynamics and trends to take place in the following key market segments. (Para. 9)

翻译：根据上述提到的关于教育指挥棒的观点，我们认为对学校、教师、学生、教育工作的评价体系会在以下方面发生一些变化。

_____

_____

5) Nevertheless, online education is an irresistible trend, and customer acquisition costs should fall drastically in the short term. (Para. 13)

翻译：然而，教育信息化是不可逆转的潮流，而且从长期来看人才培养模式将进行更新。

_____

_____

Ⅲ Discourse Practice

Read the following news and write down the main idea at the beginning of each of the paragraphs as indicated.

How Will COVID-19 Impact Global Education?

More than 60 countries in Africa, Asia, Europe, North America and South America have announced or implemented school and university closures. Indeed, the impact of COVID-19 on education has gone far beyond school closure. What is its impact on the global education landscape? How will it change the future of education in the aftermath?

1) _____. The component of health, life and well-being in curriculum varies from country to country. It is also delivered in varied ways in classrooms and schools, as a standalone course, or integrated with physical education and mental well-being. Health emergency response is often absent either in curriculum or in school activities in many countries. Now almost all the governments and education authorities are producing guidelines and guidance to the students with proper measures and actions to avoid infection and stay safe in the case of virus infection. Health education, especially those relating to emergency response will be an integral part of curriculum and school administration in the future.

2) _____. A record number of students in the world now rely on online education to continue their study due to COVID-19 quarantine and school closures. This is effective when national portals are available. Typically, China has created a national portal that can accommodate 50 million students learning online simultaneously. The outbreak has de facto accelerated the integration of technology and artificial intelligence in education. Nonetheless, lack of access to technology or good Internet connectivity could also constrain access to learning for those from disadvantaged areas or families. The disparity and inequity is likely to enlarge.

3) _____. The number of foreign students engaged in tertiary education programs worldwide has expanded massively in the past few decades, according to the OECD, rising from 2 million in 1998 to 5.3 million in 2017, of which, according to UNESCO, 2.5 million are studying outside their home region. Due to travel restrictions

imposed by many governments, many students could not return to campus as scheduled, or they have to leave the campuses during the closure of universities and colleges. Online courses are offered for many students in many institutions, but not all.

How effectively students can learn depends on how schools and teachers can manage their learning. People were used to classroom-based lectures that have been critiqued as old mode for industrial society. Indeed the outbreak forced a leap into alternative approaches to learning with integration of technology and artificial intelligence. It demands new methods and strategies of learning assessment. The key to effective evaluation lies in cognitive and brain science that could identify solutions to effective learning. Learning science will play a larger role in future educational development.

4) _____. For many students who study online due to imposed social distancing, travel restriction or school closure, home turns into a classroom, and parents enter into the role of teaching assistant or learning partner whether they're prepared or not. Many parents struggle to perform this task, especially those with limited education and resources. On the other hand, working parents tend to leave children unattended, which may lead to varied quality of learning or even risky behavior. This warrants a close parent-school partnership as well as strong and supportive parental education, which has never been more important to the learning system than right now.

5) _____. The outbreak, especially for those who have close contact with confirmed cases or experienced the death of a family member or friend, is a traumatic experience for children and young people. Stress and depression might increase as a result of a lack of social contact that used to occur through social activity and human interaction in schools. Social isolation, in the case of social distancing and school closure, might be compounded by anxiety arising from challenges with the new mode of online learning. Overall, the battle against coronavirus is a test of courage and perseverance for both individuals and nations. This has made mental well-being and mental consultancy one of the fundamental education elements in schools.

6) _____. When China was first hit by coronavirus, people in many countries offered their help in various ways—in kind, in resource and in spirit. As those countries have fallen into crisis, China has reciprocated their support. Solidarity is the key to fighting

against the global pandemic, and education lies at its core by teaching the youth to value peace and solidarity rather than conflict and division. As the preamble of the UNESCO Constitution states, "since wars begin in the minds of men, it is in the minds of men that the defenses of peace must be constructed."

With economic and social costs, and even a human toll, 7) _____. It has awakened people's awareness of many under-addressed issues and pushed many things ahead of the agenda of many governments. Evidently, education that encompasses physical, social and emotional well-being is key to sustainable development; technology and artificial intelligence have opened up new perspectives and strategies to education delivery, yet inequity will persist or even exacerbate without effective intervention by governments; and cognitive science could bring more positive changes to effective learning.

Above all, only when we educate children and youth to devote to peace and sustainable development can human beings assure a sustainable future for themselves and the planet. Sweet are the uses of adversity. Hopefully, with all these lessons learned, we can embrace a better future for education and for mankind.

Produce

Prepare for a Presentation About the Impact of COVID-19 on China's Online Education with PowerPoint Slides

1 Recap of the Previous Sessions

In Pretest, you've learned some basics about China's online education. In Prepare/Probe, you've gained a basic understanding of the development of China's education industry against the backdrop of COVID-19. In Practice, you've familiarized yourself with the necessary language points, as well as the use of graphics and the listing of main points in presentations. Now it's time to consider the design of PowerPoint slides to illustrate the impact of COVID-19 on China's online education.

⬛ The Importance of Learning How to Design PowerPoint Slides

PowerPoint is probably the most popular means of presentation now. A document is not finished only with the text part. As a professional communicator, you need to consider how you can make your document appealing to the readers' eyes. The slides are easy to prepare, and effective in presenting information. However, poorly used PPT skills are not rare in presentations. Some are due to lack of skills, while others are due to apprying too many skills. It is often said that style is a personal issue; however, in the case of presentation, legibility comes always first and should never be sacrificed for the sake of the presenter's artistic fantasies. PPT creation and decoration is not strange to most of us. Therefore, the technical part is not introduced here. Rather, this section is devoted to discussing some guidelines in using the PPT skills.

⬛ Basic Principles of Designing PowerPoint Slides

PowerPoint design can sometimes directly influence the quality of your presentation. There are various skills in its creation and decoration. The following points outlined will aid you in the process of putting together the different slide elements.

1. Choose a background that will be comfortable for your audience

As a rule, choose a design template with a light or white background. The popularity of dark templates is mostly a relic from the use of 35-mm slides, which projected badly through low-lumen equipment. Dark backgrounds blocked most of the weak light, making the bits that got through the light areas (white or yellow type and lines) appear brighter. Those low-light systems required projection in dark rooms, which challenged the way human eyes are designed to function, much like early personal computer monitors that had gray backgrounds and amber or lime green type. That caused users to develop headaches, which went away when they started using software that allowed white pages with dark type.

2. Use texts that can be read easily

One factor in readability for slides is the amount you expect viewers to read; keep in mind that they can't read and listen to you at the same time. Make their job a matter of looking quickly at the slide so they can turn their attention back to you.

Give every slide a unique title, and avoid at all cost full sentences anywhere else on the slide. For bullet points, optimally reduce each point to six words or less. If you decide to leave full sentences on your conclusions and recommendations slides, consider putting only one conclusion or recommendation per slide. (If you have a recommendation relevant to each conclusion, you might put the conclusion and the associated recommendation together.)

The following pictures show how to make texts legible and concise by improving the page layout. Instead of listing four bullet points in the original slide, the improved version put one point on a slide. They get rid of the overdone, irrelevant template. And they each add an illustration, which stands on its own. Audiences can integrate one point at a time more easily than four. They remember it better, too. The slide is simpler, so it has more impact.

Original:

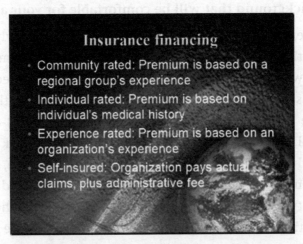

Revision:

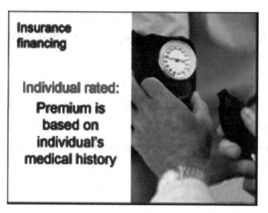

Layout 1   Layout 2

3. **Use clear, readable graphics**

Graphics are effective means in revealing data. There are different kinds of graphics: tables, pie charts, bar charts, line charts, flow charts, schedule charts, and organization charts, to name some of them. They serve different functions, and have specific advantages and shortcomings. The purpose to learn the design of each graphic is to know when to use which type of chart to fully bring out the value of your data.

For example, you may use the following chart to illustrate market segmentation.

OFFERINGS TO CUSTOMERS

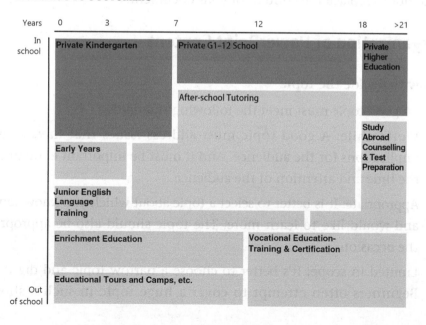

But remember, in a presentation, the audience may have only a few seconds to study the graphic (and no polite way to stop you while they try to figure out the graphic), so your job is to make the graphics as clear and easy to interpret as you can.

On any slide that has a graphic, fill up most of the available space with the graphic. Make the graphic big enough so that the accompanying text does not overwhelm the image. Text within a graphic—axis labels, curve or data point labels, and any other "incidental" letters or numbers you might include—should be at least 14-point, and in most fonts 16-point is usually preferable, even on the axis labels.

4. Use subtle animation to help readers focus

Animation can be especially helpful in a presentation to emphasize a point. For example, you can show a table of all the software in the mooring-system project that ends on the total amount of time to run all of the separate programs, but then let the new simulator and its run time appear later. That way, the audience will listen to what you have to say about the other programs before they see how much better the simulator is. Be aware that animation run amok can be more distracting than helpful, but animation used carefully and intentionally can help keep your audience's attention and point them to significant features on the slide.

Finally, it's important to remember that any visual technique is there to aid, not to replace the content of your document.

Ⅳ Organization of PowerPoint Content

1. How to decide the topic

A good topic must meet the following standards:

- Worthwhile: A good topic must address issues that have significant implications for the audience. And it must be important enough to merit the time and attention of the audience.

- Appropriate: It is better to select a topic about which you know something and would like to learn more. The topic should also be appropriate for the occasion.

- Limited in scope: It's better to choose a narrow topic and dig it deeper. Beginners often attempt to cover a huge topic in such a short time that nothing specific is covered, say, everything is touched on but only superficially.

In this chapter, you need to present the impact of COVID-19 on China's online education. That is a large topic and you need to narrow it down, and different topics come into your mind: the impact of COVID-19 on Chinese family education; the impact of COVID-19 on Chinese training market; how COVID-19 impacts Chinese students' ways of learning; how Chinese students can adjust to online learning during COVID-19, etc.

You may make a survey in your class and read the passage on Pages 84–90 intensively to decide the most suitable topic. After the survey and reading, you decide to talk about the trend of China's online education in the post-pandemic era.

2. **How to present the introductory part**

1) In the introductory part, you need to figure out how to get your audience's attention. Generally speaking, the following methods can be used:

- Ask questions. You may say:

  _____

  _____

- Use a quotation. You may say:

  _____

  _____

- Tell a (personal) story. You may say:

  _____

  _____

- Use parallelism. You may say:

  _____

  _____

- Illustrate an amazing or shocking fact (or showing startling statistics). You may say:

  _____

- Make the topic relevant to your audience. You may say:

_____

_____

2) After capturing their attention, you need to reveal your topic and preview the body of the speech. For this topic, your main body part can be:

_____

_____

3. How to present the body part

In the body part, you need to pay special attention to the following elements:

1) Main points

- Be related to the central idea. The topic is about China's online education, so talking about the education of other countries would be off topic.

- Be independent of each other. If the first main point is political influences, the second point can be economic or macro-environment influences. If the second point is the impact of government intervention, then it is not independent of the first main point.

2) Supporting materials

- Follow the main points. In the passage, after stating graduate admission test preparation segment will regain momentum, the author offers supporting examples by saying "Online training providers, such as TAL Online, Zuoyebang, and Yuanfudao, have all reported more than 20 million new users during the past six weeks."

- Include examples, statistics and testimony. As the passage abounds in examples, statistics and testimony, your presentation should also present as such to be more convincing. For instance, you can cite the opinion from online training providers: Ma Xiaoping, CEO of TopSchools, noted that online education has been pushed to the foreground by the pandemic, attracting much attention to the industry.

3) Transitions and signposts

- Cite examples. You may use phrases like _for example, as an illustration, according to statistics,_ etc. When talking about the influence of political elements, the passage mentions policies in Shandong and Guangdong. In your presentation, you may analyze relevant education policies issued by the local government.

- Introduce a different opinion. You may use phrases like *but, however, on the contrary, by comparison*, etc. In the passage, we can see lots of sentences introducing a different opinion. For instance, "the COVID-19 outbreak may change the teaching venue in the short term, but its impact on tuition and student enrollment is negligible." In your presentation, you may also use this method. For example, after saying "Online education may work for adults willing to learn something new and to improve themselves", you may introduce a different opinion by saying "but most of the young students in China are passive learners, who can only take in knowledge when teachers are around."

- Introduce the result. You may use phrases like *as a result, as such, consequently, therefore*, etc. In your presentation, when introducing the influence or the result, you may also utilize such words. For instance, you may say: "Some students are more productive in the evening, so they tend to organize their studies before and after dinner."

- Show order. You may use words and phrases like *first, after that, next, in the meantime, last, finally, then*, etc.

4. How to present the concluding part

You need to follow two major guidelines in the concluding part:

1) Let the audience know that you are going to end your speech.

2) Reinforce your main ideas of the speech. The following methods can be used:

- Summarize your speech into several points. You may say:

_____

_____

- Use a quotation. You may say:

_____

_____

- Refer back to the introduction. You may say:

_____

• Call for action. You may say:

_____

• Make a prediction or recommendation. You may say:

_____

_____

• Make a dramatic statement. You may say:

_____

_____

5. Tips on how to make a good presentation

1) Preparation, preparation, and preparation.

2) Think about the audience.

• Think why the presentation is important to them and how they benefit.

3) Communication.

• Presentation should be a two-way communication.

• Make the audience engaged.

• Look at them, speak to them, ask rhetorical questions, and use short pauses.

• Do not hide behind a computer, a paper or a desk.

4) Prepare the little things.

• Address your audience appropriately.

• Use specific terms to describe what is on your PowerPoint slides.

• Show a picture, a graph, a table or a chart.

5) Structure your presentation.

6) Do not read or read like you mean it.

7) Nonverbal communication is also important, so your eye contact, facial expressions, stance and so on also matter.

8) Pay attention to PowerPoint slide design.

• Do not put all the information on the PowerPoint slides.

- Do not overload your PowerPoint slides with texts and read the texts to them.

9) Practice, practice, practice.

10) Do not forget to thank the audience at the end and leave question time if possible.

Post-Learning Evaluation

No.	Statements	Strongly agree	Agree	Not sure	Disagree	Strongly disagree
1	I have grasped the expressions related to the theme.					
2	I am familiar with the key words and phrases in the passage.					
3	I understand the major points of the passage.					
4	I am familiar with the terms explained in the footnotes.					
5	I am able to list main points clearly in an English presentation.					
6	I know how to properly use graphics in a presentation.					
7	I am able to follow the key principles of designing PowerPoint slides and organizing PowerPoint content.					
8	I am able to design visual aids and organize the content when assigned to.					
9	I am able to analyze China's online education from different aspects.					
10	I have improved my teamwork and collaboration skills in finishing the tasks together with my team members.					

No.	Statements	Strongly agree	Agree	Not sure	Disagree	Strongly disagree
11	I am aware that China's online education is capturing the attention of overseas institutes and organizations.					
12	As an online learner I realize that online education is flourishing in China.					
13	I take pride in China's rapid development in online education.					
14	I predict that online education will accelerate the spread of Chinese culture to other countries and regions.					
15	I am more motivated to introduce China's online education in my own way to international friends.					

Chapter 5

Chinese Scientists

Pretest

How much do you know about Chinese scientists? Can you match the books or inventions with their authors or inventors? You may go to our MOOC (Chapter 5 Science and Technology) to learn more before taking this quiz.

1) Daming Calendar   (   ) A. Zhang Heng

2) *Meng Xi Bi Tan*   (   ) B. Li Shizhen

3) Houfeng Seismometer   (   ) C. Tu Youyou

4) *The Compendium of Materia Medica*   (   ) D. Shen Kuo

5) dihydroartemisinin   (   ) E. Zu Chongzhi

Pretask

You are currently working as an intern of the Artemisinin Research Center, China Academy of Chinese Medical Sciences, and the center has been invited to attend an international conference. Your leader has assigned you to make a brochure about the center to help other people know more about it.

1) To accomplish the task, I plan to take the following steps:

                                                     .

For the first step, I think _____

might be challenging.

For the second step, I think _____

might be challenging.

_____

_____

2) I expect to achieve the following goals after learning the unit:

_____

_____

Passage

The Discovery of Artemisinin and Nobel Prize in Physiology or Medicine[1]

This article is adapted from an article published in Science China—Life Sciences[2] *(2015). Professor Tu Youyou is the first female Chinese scientist to receive the Nobel Prize. The following passage is an objective description about how the Nobel Prize winner Professor Tu Youyou discovered artemisinin and why she was awarded the Nobel Prize.*

1   The discovery of artemisinin dramatically changes the landscape to combat malaria and leads to a **paradigm** shift in antimalarial drug development. According to a recent WHO[3] report, between 2000 and 2012, the malaria incidence rates were reduced by 25% globally, and the global malaria **mortality** rate was reduced by 42% during the same period. Many countries are now on track for declaring

paradigm /ˈpærədaɪm/
n. a typical example or pattern of sth.

mortality /mɔːˈtæləti/
n. the number of deaths in a particular situation or period of time

---

1   The Nobel Prize in Physiology or Medicine is awarded yearly by the Nobel Assembly at the Karolinska Institute for outstanding discoveries in physiology or medicine.

2   *Science China—Life Sciences* is a monthly journal supervised by the Chinese Academy of Sciences, focusing on significant, innovative, and cutting-edge research results in a wide range of areas in life sciences.

3   WHO, the World Health Organization, established on April 7, 1948, is a specialized agency of the United Nations responsible for international public health. It is headquartered in Geneva, Switzerland, with six semi-autonomous regional offices and 150 field offices worldwide.

derivative /dɪˈrɪvətɪv/
n. a word or thing that has been developed or produced from another word or thing

avert /əˈvɜːt/
v. to prevent sth. bad or dangerous from happening

parasite /ˈpærəsaɪt/
n. a small animal or plant that lives on or inside another animal or plant and gets its food from it

infection /ɪnˈfekʃn/
n. the act or process of causing or getting a disease

malaria-free status. Artemisinin and its **derivatives** have played a key role in malaria related mortality. According to a recent estimate, approximately 22% of the 663 million **averted** clinical cases were due to the use of artemisinin combination therapies (ACTs, 青蒿素联合疗法).

2 Artemisinin represents a new class of antimalarial drugs, which leads to two paradigm shifts in antimalarial research and therapy. The first one is the change from quinoline (喹啉) -based antimalarial drugs to artemisinin-based therapies due to the emergence of **parasites** resistant to quinoline drugs. Currently, ACTs are the drugs recommended by WHO for treating the deadly plasmodium falciparum (恶性疟原虫) **infections** and are being used worldwide. The second paradigm shift is the change of research direction in antimalarial drug development. Artemisinin and its derivatives are in a new class of antimalarial agents with unique structure, which has become a new direction for antimalarial drug development. For example, some of the most promising drugs under clinical trials, including OZ277 and OZ439, are synthetic peroxides (过氧化物) with key structures similar to artemisinin. Additionally, research related to artemisinin has been a hot topic in malaria and other fields such as antiviral and anticancer treatment in the past 15 years. A search of PubMed[4] for key word "artemisinin" identified 2,869 articles published in the last three years. The discovery of artemisinin changes the directions on how we treat malaria and how we develop and search for new antimalarial drugs. The impacts on global health and the paradigm shifts in antimalarial drug research are the key factors

---

4 PubMed is a free search engine accessing primarily the MEDLINE database of references and abstracts on life sciences and biomedical topics.

that the Nobel Committee considered when they evaluated all the **nominations**.

A Brief History of Artemisinin Discovery

3 Artemisinin was discovered in the 1970s. In response to a request from the Vietnam government for help on malaria treatment, the Chinese government launched an operation called 523 Project. On May 23, 1967, a meeting was held in Beijing Hotel to discuss plans for the search, which officially launched the project. Professor Tu was brought into the project in January, 1969 and was appointed as a team leader to search for Chinese **herb**[5] **recipes** having antimalarial activities.

4 Professor Tu's group started with a search for recipes that had been used to treat fever. They searched more than 2,000 recipes and **compiled** 640 recipes for further evaluation within three months. They then looked at the individual plant names that had high frequencies of appearance in the recipes. Artemisia annua (青蒿) was one of the plants that appeared in the recipes frequently. Professor Tu's group tested **extracts** from more than 100 plants on **rodent** malaria parasite plasmodium berghei (伯氏疟原虫). An extract from artemisia annua had about 68% inhibition rate initially, but the activity was not stable, varying from 12% to 40% inhibition in subsequent repeats. The variation in antimalarial activity could be due to many factors, including geographic origins of the plant, seasonal variation, different parts of the plant (leaves or stem) and the methods used in

---

5 Chinese herb mainly refers to the medicine used to prevent or treat diseases in traditional Chinese medicine, which can be divided into three categories according to raw materials: plants, minerals and animals.

nomination
/ˌnɒmɪ'neɪʃn/
n. the act of officially naming a candidate

herb /hɜːb/
n. a plant whose leaves, flowers or seeds are used to flavor food, in medicines or for their pleasant smell

recipe /'resəpi/
n. a method or an idea that seems likely to have a particular result

compile /kəm'paɪl/
v. to produce a book, list, report, etc. by bringing together different items, articles, songs, etc.; to collect information in order to produce a book, list, etc.

extract /'ekstrækt/
n. a substance that has been obtained from sth. else using a particular process

rodent /'rəʊdnt/
n. any small animal that belongs to a group of animals with strong sharp front teeth

instability /ɪnstə'bɪləti/
n. the quality or state of being likely to change or fail suddenly

inhibit /ɪn'hɪbɪt/
v. to prevent sth. from happening or make it happen more slowly or less frequently than normal

synthesis /'sɪnθəsɪs/
n. the natural chemical production of a substance in animals and plants

extraction. One day, Professor Tu was reading some recipes written by Ge Hong[6] around 1,700 years ago. In one of his recipes, Ge Hong described how to obtain "juice" from Qinghao (artemisia annua) plant to treat fever by using cold water, instead of the traditional methods of boiling herbs for preparing Chinese medicines. Professor Tu suddenly realized that high temperature could be the cause of **instability** in antimalarial activity they experienced. The second hint Professor Tu had from Ge Hong's description was that the plant leaf was likely the part having the most activity because the "juice" could be obtained from the leaves much easier than other parts of the plant. She decided to use ether (乙醚), replacing ethanol (乙醇), to extract the active ingredients from the plant leaves and obtained sample #191 that could **inhibit** rodent and monkey malaria with 100% activity on October 4, 1971. Professor Tu presented her work at a meeting held in Nanjing on March 8, 1972. Her results were exciting, and the leadership of the 523 Project decided that she should conduct a clinical trial in the same year. In August 1972, Professor Tu led a clinical trial team to Hainan Island and tested her extracts on 21 patients, achieving 95% to 100% inhibition after taking the medicine herself to evaluate the safety of the extract. Professor Tu reported the results from the clinical trials in a meeting held on November 17, 1972. The exciting results led to a large-scale, countrywide effort to extract large quantities of the pure ingredient (or artemisinin crystal) to determine its chemical structure and **synthesis** involving a large number of scientists from many institutions.

---

6 Ge Hong (283–363), also called "Baopuzi", was a famous Daoist, alchemist and medical scientist in the East Jin Dynasty. His book, *A Handbook of Prescriptions for Emergencies*, or *Zhou Hou Bei Ji Fang*, is one of the greatest medical works in traditional Chinese medicine.

Major Contributions Professor Tu Made to the Discovery of Artemisinin

5   **Bringing the plant into the 523 Project.** Hundreds of scientists **were involved in** the 523 Project, however, Professor Tu was the person who brought artemisia annua into the 523 Project or rediscovered the plant. In a 523 meeting summary dated June 1, 1971, the scientists of the 523 Project discussed progress, including the identification of different herbs/plants with antimalarial activities, but did not mention the artemisia annua plant, suggesting that they **were** not **aware of** the antimalarial activity of the artemisia annua plant at that time (or it was not among their priorities). Nine months later on March 8, 1972, Professor Tu described her discovery of extract from artemisia annua and showed that the extract was effective in treating plasmodium berghei at another 523 Project meeting held in Nanjing. These two classified 523 documents clearly showed that Professor Tu was the person who brought artemisia annua into the 523 Project.

6   **Discovering a method to extract active ingredient.** In her presentation dated March 8, 1972, Professor Tu described a procedure for extracting stable and active antimalarial extract (neutral portion). They replaced ethanol (boiling point 78 °C) with ether (35 °C boiling point) in the extraction, which greatly improved the stability of the active ingredient. Other groups in the 523 Project were able to obtain high quality of artemisinin crystals after hearing her report. There were two letters sent to Tu's institute (Yunnan Institute of Pharmacy and Shandong Institute of Parasitology) in 1973 that expressed **gratitude** for sharing information on artemisinin extraction. A copy of each letter can be found in the book titled *Qinghao and Qinghaosu*

be involved in
   to take part in sth.; to be part of sth. or connected with sth.

be aware of
   to know or realize sth.

gratitude /ˈɡrætɪtjuːd/
n. the feeling of being grateful and wanting to express your thanks

smear /smɪə(r)/
n. a thin tissue or blood sample spread on a glass slide and stained for cytologic examination and diagnosis under a microscope

set off
to start a process or series of events

dosage /ˈdəʊsɪdʒ/
n. an amount of sth., usually a medicine or a drug, that is taken regularly over a particular period of time

solubility /ˌsɒljuˈbɪləti/
n. the quality of being soluble and easily dissolved in liquid

efficacy /ˈefɪkəsi/
n. the ability of sth., especially a drug or a medical treatment, to produce the results that are wanted

Derivative Drugs. Therefore, Professor Tu was the person who discovered an efficient method for extracting the active ingredient from the artemisia annua plant.

7   **Conducting the first clinical trial of artemisia extract in human patients.** Professor Tu also led a team to Hainan and conducted the first clinical trial in humans in August 1972. They tested the drug in 11 cases of plasmodium vivax (间日症原虫), 9 cases of plasmodium falciparum, and 1 case of a mixed infection. All the patients quickly returned to normal temperature from 40 °C, and many were negative of parasites in the blood **smear**. The results were better than the control group given chloroquine (氯喹 [一 种疟疾特效药]). Later, they tested another 9 cases in Beijing and obtained similar results. She wrote a report and presented the results in a 523 meeting held on November 17, 1972, **setting off** a large-scale effort to isolate the active ingredient. Thus, Professor Tu was the person who conducted the first successful clinical trial in human using artemisia extract.

8   **Isolation of active ingredient for structural studies.** Following the demonstration of antimalarial activity, her group continued to isolate active ingredient of white crystal that had melting point of 156–157 °C on November 8, 1972, which they named Qinghaosu. They showed that 50–100 mg/kg **dosages** could cure rodent malaria parasites. The isolation of the crystal allowed further investigation of its chemical structure. She also coordinated with scientists in Beijing and Shanghai and played a role in determining the structure using the crystal that they obtained.

9   **Discovering dihydroartemisinin** (双氢青蒿素). Professor Tu also discovered dihydroartemisinin that greatly improved water **solubility** and treatment **efficacy**.

National and International Recognition

10   Because of her critical contributions and achievements in the discovery, Professor Tu received numerous awards at home and abroad, including National Model Worker[7] by the State Council in 1995, the 2011 Lasker DeBakey Clinical[8] Medical Research Award, the 2015 Nobel Prize in Physiology or Medicine, and more.

Credits and Controversies

11   **As to** Professor Tu Youyou's credits and contributions to the 523 Project and the discovery of artemisinin, there might have been some other voices. It is a fact that a large number of people **took part in** and contributed to the project. However, all other later work was based on her initial demonstration of active ingredient from the Qinghao plant. Without her initial presentation on March 8, 1972, there would have had no Qinghao crystals obtained by other institutes, no work on chemical structure, no artemisinin derivatives synthesized, and no related clinical trials. Often when multiple people are involved in an important research development, the Nobel Prize Committee[9] recognizes only the individual who made the **seminal** discovery that led to the development. For example, the Nobel Prize

controversy
/ˈkɒntrəvɜːsi/
n. public discussion and argument about sth. that many people strongly disagree about, think is bad, or are shocked by
as to
   as for; about
take part in
   to be involved in sth.

seminal /ˈsemɪnl/
adj. very important and having a strong influence on later developments

---

7 National Model Worker is an honorary title awarded by the State Council to exemplary vanguards in the construction of socialist material civilization, political civilization and spiritual civilization of China.

8 Lasker DeBakey Clinical Medical Research Award has been awarded annually since 1945 to living persons who have made major contributions to medical science or who have performed public service on behalf of medicine. They are administered by the Lasker Foundation, founded by Albert Lasker and his wife Mary Woodard Lasker (later a medical research activist).

9 Nobel Prize Committee is a working body responsible for most of the work involved in selecting Nobel Prize laureates.

went to Harald Zur Hausen for the discovery of the papillomavirus (乳头瘤病毒) in cervical cancer (宫颈癌) and not to others who later developed the **vaccine**.

vaccine /'væksiːn/
n. a substance that is put into the blood and that protects the body from a disease

Conclusions

12   There is no doubt that Professor Tu (her group) is the first person who brought the artemisia annua into the 523 Project, the first person who obtained the active ingredient (extract and crystal), and the first person who demonstrated antimalarial activity in human. The impact of artemisinin on public health is immediate and tremendous. Millions of lives have been saved by the use of artemisinin. Additionally, the discovery of artemisinin has led to paradigm shifts in antimalarial research and therapy. There are few scientific discoveries that have the same scale and instant impacts on public health, human productivity, and scientific research as artemisinin has.

(1,685 words)

Theme-Related Words & Expressions

paradigm shift	范式转移
antimalarial	抗疟疾的
drug development	药物开发
incidence rate	发病率
mortality rate	死亡率
clinical case	临床病例
clinical trial	临床试验
treat	治疗
Chinese herb	中草药
activity	活性
extract	提取物

inhibition	抑制
fever	发热
active ingredient	活性成分
negative	阴性
blood smear	血液涂片
control group	控制组；实验对照组
isolate	分离
structural study	结构分析
melting point	熔点
dosage	剂量
water solubility	水溶性
treatment efficacy	疗效
Nobel Prize in Physiology or Medicine	诺贝尔生理学或医学奖

Prepare/Probe

❶ Reading Comprehension

Decide whether the following statements are true or false according to the passage. Write T for true and F for false.

1) Artemisinin and its derivatives contributed to a 42% mortality rate drop around the world between 2000 and 2012. (   )

2) Artemisinin gave rise to significant changes in antimalaria drug development and antimalaria therapy. (   )

3) Professor Tu didn't participate in the 523 Project at the beginning. (   )

4) It was from traditional Chinese medicine that Professor Tu got the inspiration to use ether to extract the active ingredients from the leaves of artemisia annua. (   )

5) Professor Tu won the Nobel Prize in Physiology or Medicine because she discovered artemisinin that saved millions of lives all by herself. (   )

❶ Structure Building

Check your understanding of the overall structure of the passage by completing the following diagram.

The Significance of the Discovery	
The significance of the discovery of artemisinin (Paras. 1–2)	The discovery of artemisinin has dramatically changed the 1) _____ situation in the world and resulted in 2) _____ in antimalarial drug development.

The Discovery of Artemisinin	
A brief history of the discovery of artemisinin (Paras. 3–4)	The Chinese government 3)_____ the 523 Project in order to help a neighboring country in 1967.
	• Professor Tu joined the project and set out to search for ways to cure malaria from 4) _____ in 1969. • Inspired by Ge Hong, Professor Tu and her team successfully 5) _____ sample #191 in 1971. • Professor Tu conducted the first clinical trial of artemisia extracts in humans, including herself, 6) _____ the safety of the extracts in 1972.
Professor Tu's contributions (Paras. 5–9)	• She was the first person to bring the plant 7) _____ into the 523 Project. • She found a better way to 8) _____ the active ingredient from the plant by using ether. • She finished the first clinical trial in humans using artemisia extracts. • She and her group isolated the active ingredient to make 9) _____ of its chemical structure possible. • She discovered dihydroartemisinin that greatly 10) _____ water solubility and treatment efficacy.

Continued

Influence	
National and international recognition (Para. 10)	• Professor Tu received numerous awards 11) ___ _____ due to her contributions to and achievements in the discovery of artemisinin.
Credits and controversies (Para. 11)	• There existed some controversies about the discovery of artemisinin. However, there is no doubt that Professor Tu played a(n) 12) _____ role in the process.
Conclusions	
Conclusions (Para. 12)	• Professor Tu made great contributions to the discovery of artemisinin, which has 13) _____ on public health.

Practice

❶ Vocabulary Practice

1. **Match the following theme-related words in Column A with their Chinese equivalents in Column B.**

Column A	Column B
1) isolate	A. 合成
2) avert	B. 感染
3) synthesis	C. 避免
4) derivative	D. 死亡率
5) treatment efficacy	E. 提取物
6) extract	F. 分离
7) infection	G. 疫苗
8) inhibit	H. 疗效
9) mortality rate	I. 处方

10) recipe   J. 发病率

11) incidence rate   K. 衍生物

12) vaccine   L. 禁止

2. **Fill in the blanks with the words or phrases in the box. Change the form if necessary.**

extract	in response to	gratitude	avert	efficacy
inhibit	be on track	seminal	coordinate	derivative

1) If you are not professionals, you should be really careful when you invest in financial products and their _____.

2) You should express your _____ to them so long as they are willing to help you.

3) The path to success is a strategic route, and it should _____ from the beginning.

4) Positive emotions facilitate the creative aspects of learning and negative emotions _____ them.

5) Different _____ may be obtained if different extraction methods are used in traditional Chinese medicine.

6) Recent medical studies confirm the _____ of a healthier lifestyle.

7) Under the current international economic circumstances, all parties should cooperate and _____ with each other.

8) Textbooks are tools to educate students in virtue; therefore, it is a(n) _____ step to explore and use Chinese textbooks loaded with traditional virtues.

9) There is mounting evidence that the frequency and magnitude of landsliding is changing in many parts of the world _____ climate change.

10) There are inexpensive steps that can help _____ this kind of accidents.

🔢 Sentence Practice

Study the sentence structure first, and then translate each of the given Chinese sentences into English by imitating the sentence structure.

1) The variation in antimalarial activity could be due to many factors, including geographic origins of the plant, seasonal variation, different parts of the plant (leaves or stem) and the methods used in extraction. (Para. 4)

   翻译：中国传统文化在全球流行可能有许多原因，包括中国传统文化的包容性和中华民族的文化自信。

   _____

   _____

2) In one of his recipes, Ge Hong described how to obtain "juice" from Qinghao (artemisia annua) plant to treat fever by using cold water, instead of the traditional methods of boiling herbs for preparing Chinese medicines. (Para. 4)

   翻译：坚持房子是用来住的、不是用来炒的定位，加快建立多主体供给、多渠道保障、租购并举的住房制度。

   _____

   _____

3) Without her initial presentation on March 8, 1972, there would have had no Qinghao crystals obtained by other institutes, no work on chemical structure, no artemisinin derivatives synthesized, and no related clinical trials. (Para. 11)

   翻译：没有一代代中国人坚持不懈的努力和付出，就不会有国家的强盛和中华民族的伟大复兴。

   _____

   _____

4) There is no doubt that Professor Tu (her group) is the first person who brought the artemisia annua into the 523 Project, the first person who obtained the active ingredient (extract and crystal), and the first person who demonstrated antimalarial activity in human. (Para. 12)

翻译：毫无疑问，苏炳添是第一位百米跑进10秒的亚洲本土运动员，第一位夺得钻石联赛百米冠军的亚洲人，第一位进入奥运会百米决赛的亚洲人。

5) There are few scientific discoveries <u>that</u> have the same scale and instant impacts on public health, human productivity, and scientific research <u>as</u> artemisinin has. (Para. 12)

翻译：很少有新技术能像移动支付这样彻底改变人们的生活方式和行为习惯。

⩩ Discourse Practice

1. **Complete the fragments with the suitable words from the box, and then sequence the fragments in the correct order. You may not use any of the words more than once.**

for	as	which	also	when	by	first	therefore

A. In 1973, Professor Tu wanted to confirm the carbonyl group in the artemisinin molecule; _____ she accidentally synthesized dihydroartemisinin.

B. In 1972, she and her colleagues obtained the pure substance and named it Qinghaosu, or artemisinin _____ it is commonly called in the West, _____ has saved millions of lives, especially in the developing world.

C. _____ her work, she was awarded the Nobel Prize in Physiology or Medicine on October 5, 2015.

D. _____ 1971, her team had made 380 extracts from 200 herbs, and discovered that the extracts from artemisia annua looked particularly promising in dramatically inhibiting plasmodium growth in animals. Professor Tu found an effective way to extract it and her innovations boosted potency and slashed toxicity of this extract.

E. Professor Tu Youyou started her malaria research in China _____ the "Cultural Revolution" was in progress.

F. Professor Tu _____ studied the chemical structure and pharmacology of artemisinin. Her group _____ determined the chemical structure of artemisinin.

G. In early 1969, Professor Tu was appointed head of the 523 Project research group at her institute. She collected 2,000 candidate recipes, ancient texts, and folk remedies for possible leads for her research.

Sequence: _____

Produce

Make a Brochure About the Artemisinin Research Center

❶ Recap of the Previous Sessions

In Pretest, you've come to gain some knowledge about Chinese scientists. In Prepare/Probe, you've grasped the main idea and structure of the text. In Practice, you've familiarized yourself with some key expressions, structures, sentence patterns in the text, and some other information about Professor Tu Youyou. Therefore, it's time to consider the production of a brochure about the center where Professor Tu is working.

❷ Definition of a Brochure

A brochure is an informative paper document (often also used for advertising) that can be folded into a template, pamphlet, or leaflet. A brochure can also be a set of related unfolded papers put into a pocket folder or packet. When used in business, brochures are promotional documents, primarily used to introduce a company, organization, products or services and inform prospective customers or members of the public of the benefits.

❸ Structure of a Brochure

A brochure usually includes two parts. The first part is the heading, including a title and sometimes a subtitle. The title mainly shows the name of the organization or else introduced in the brochure. And the subtitle is usually some descriptive introductions about the subject. In some cases, below the title and subtitle, there are also contact information (details), e.g. telephone number, email, etc. The second part is the body, which introduces the subject in detail. Its content consists of foundation, history, characteristics, merits, purposes, agenda, or other related information. You can list them one by one, or just write them in ordinary essay styles.

A brochure can also be divided into three parts: the front page, the inside panel and the back page. In this way, information related to the title or the main event usually appears on the front page, detailed contents, like the main speakers of a conference, the main topics of a seminar, etc., are often listed on the inside panel and contact information is always written on the back page.

When writing a brochure, you should try to employ a concise and simplistic style because nobody likes to read a long or wordy brochure.

If possible, a photo or some photos of the object that you are writing about should be included in the brochure to make it more vivid and effective.

The brochure about a person may be somewhat different. The specific contents of a brochure about a person are listed in the following table:

Brochure	Contents
The first part	name, birthday, nationality, degrees, titles, etc.
The second part	main achievements, major honors, main credentials, etc.

Ⅳ Samples of brochures

Sample 1:

From the brochure above, we can see clearly on the front page the heading part, including the title (OHSU, MATTERS OF THE MIND, Summer Series), which informed the readers of the organizer, the event and the subtitle (As one of our special supporters, you are invited to a series of small discussions on multiple sclerosis, Parkinson's, and Alzheimer's diseases. Please join us.), which functioned as an invitation to potential attendees. On the second page, we may find the detailed arrangements, the contact and a telephone number. On Pages 3, 4 and 5, lecturers and their photos, titles and other brief introductions were given.

Sample 2:

> **Yuan Longping** (1930–2021), male, Chinese, graduated from the Southwest Agriculture Institute in 1953 with a Bachelor's Degree, internationally honored as the "Father of Hybrid Rice", a member of the Chinese Academy of Engineering and an international member of the United States National Academy of Sciences.
>
>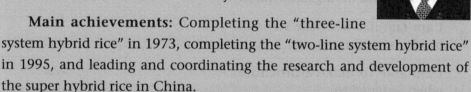
>
> **Main achievements:** Completing the "three-line system hybrid rice" in 1973, completing the "two-line system hybrid rice" in 1995, and leading and coordinating the research and development of the super hybrid rice in China.
>
> **Main honors:** The grand prize of State Award for Inventions in 1981, the first State Preeminent Science and Technology Award of China in 2001, the Wolf Prize in 2004, the World Food Prize in 2004, and the Medal of the Republic in 2019.

This sample brochure is much simpler when compared with the first one. It includes two parts: the heading part, which tells the readers the name of the main character and other details, such as a photo, the gender, the nationality, degrees, titles and positions held, etc., and the body part, which informs the readers of the main achievements and honors of the main character. This brochure uses only phrases, not sentences, thus achieving a style of simplicity.

After you have learned how to write a brochure, you may start to produce your own brochure. In reviewing your draft, you also need to check the use of tenses, personal pronouns, direct or indirect speeches, the length and the accurate delivery of the main points of your writing.

Post-Learning Evaluation

No.	Statements	Strongly agree	Agree	Not sure	Disagree	Strongly disagree
1	I have grasped the expressions related to the theme					
2	I am familiar with the key words and phrases in the passage.					
3	I understand the reasons why Professor Tu Youyou was awarded the Nobel Prize in Physiology or Medicine.					
4	I am familiar with the terms explained in the footnotes.					
5	I am familiar with the usage of linking words in English writing.					
6	I am familiar with the steps of brochure writing.					
7	I am able to make a brochure when assigned to.					
8	I have improved my teamwork and collaboration skills in finishing the tasks together with my team members.					
9	I am aware that lab experiments are also applicable to traditional Chinese medicine.					
10	I am proud of the contributions China and Chinese scientists have made to the global public health.					
11	I appreciate and admire the spirit of craftsmanship Professor Tu Youyou demonstrated in scientific research.					

Continued

No.	Statements	Strongly agree	Agree	Not sure	Disagree	Strongly disagree
12	I appreciate and admire the devotion Professor Tu Youyou demonstrated to scientific research.					
13	I appreciate and admire the pioneering efforts Professor Tu Youyou made when she did scientific research.					
14	After learning this chapter, I am more motivated to tell stories about Chinese scientists to international friends when I have the opportunity.					

Chapter **6**

Chinese Architecture

Pretest

Are you confident of introducing our Chinese architecture to the world? In the following multiple-choice questions, you need to match the features of Chinese architecture or styles of Chinese architects with correct answers. You may go to our MOOC (Chapter 7 Architecture) to learn more before taking this quiz.

1) In the Forbidden City, from south to north lie three important palaces: _____, _____, and _____, the importance of which also decreases in this sequence.

   A. Hall of Preserving Harmony

   B. Hall of Supreme Harmony

   C. Hall of Central Harmony

2) As for the ancient dwellings, the northerners are more likely to live in _____, _____, and _____, while southerners are more inclined to live in _____, _____ and _____.

   A. the cave house

   B. the hanging house

   C. the Hui-style architecture

   D. the Mongolian yurt

   E. Tianjing courtyard

   F. Siheyuan

3) The major differences between northern and southern garden architectures can be summarized as their _____, _____, and _____.

   A. architectural elements

   B. water spaces

   C. designs of space

   D. uses of color

   E. sizes

Pretask

This summer vocation you are selected as an exchange student to study a few months in an Ivy League university. At the end of your first month there, you are invited to an interview session in the university's anniversary ceremony where you are asked to interview one of the most prominent alumni, followed by an interaction session with audience where both of you are supposed to answer questions. As you are pursuing an architectural degree, you regard the following interview with Ma Yansong as an excellent example to learn from, based on which you and your partner would prepare and rehearse an interview by anticipating possible questions and answers.

1) To accomplish the task, I plan to take the following steps:

_____ .

For the first step, I think _____

might be challenging.

For the second step, I think _____

might be challenging.

_____

_____

2) I expect to achieve the following goals after learning the unit:

_____

_____

Passage

Beijing, a Future Constellation

This article is adapted from Sara Banti's article from the website of Abitare *magazine (December, 2017). It is a piece of interview between Ma Yansong, a renowned Chinese young architect and partner in MAD Architects and* Abitare, *an international architecture and design media founded in 1961. The interview heavily explored his architectural philosophies and the design logic of contemporary Beijing.*

visionary / ˈvɪʒənri /
adj. original and showing the ability to think about or plan the future with great imagination and intelligence

1   The historic core of the Chinese capital is destined to become a tourist and cultural attraction at the center of this megalopolis. In this interview, Ma Yansong[1], a partner in MAD Architects and one of the most **visionary** designers and planners around today, tells us all about this development. To the question about who has a recipe for growth, he advises us to look for inspiration in nature and traditional architecture.

2   The atmosphere is quiet and relaxing in the studio of MAD Architects in one of the liveliest districts of Beijing. The members of the team— who come from all over the world—wander around between large tables, computers and models. Trays of fruit and sweets hint at an almost family setting, and yet there are now a hundred people on the staff and

---

1   Ma Yansong, born in 1975, Beijing, China, is a Chinese architect whose designs reflected his "Shanshui City" concept, which called for balancing the natural environment, the urban landscape, and society in new ways through architecture.

it's getting **cramped** under the wooden trusses of this well-lit former printing works. In a few months they'll be moving to the eighth and last floor of a building not far away, from which, they tell me, it is possible to see the Forbidden City. We have come to meet Ma Yansong, founder of the practice, to get the opinion of one of the most brilliant architects of his generation about the future of this fascinating capital, which is **steeped** in history but also in contradictions. The occasion for this is provided by the very recent opening of Chaoyang Park Plaza[2], a complex of over 200,000 square meters designed by MAD that manages to fit two office towers, low buildings with shops and a residential condominium onto a rectangular lot in Sanlitun, one of the most commercial areas of Beijing.

3　*With its organic forms, its shiny black surfaces and the **evanescent** effect produced by the **tinted** glass, Chaoyang Park Plaza seems to remind us of Batman's Gotham City[3]. Could this recent project of yours be said to convey a vision of Beijing today?*

4　The initial inspiration came from traditional Shanshui paintings[4], which represent natural landscapes. But I didn't want to be agreeable with this project. I am highly critical of the architecture that has developed in the district, with its multi-colored boxes in an

---

2　Chaoyang Park Plaza is a mixed-use development constructed in the central business district of Beijing, China. The 120m-high plaza comprises over 20,000 m² of commercial, office and residential space.

3　Gotham City is the home of Batman. Batman's place of residence was first identified as Gotham City in *Batman 4* (comic book released in winter, 1940).

4　Shanshui painting refers to a style of Chinese painting that involves the painting of scenery or natural landscapes with brush and ink. The name literally translates to "mountain-water-picture". Mountains, rivers, and often waterfalls are prominent in this art form. Shanshui painting first rose to wide prominence in China in the tenth and eleventh centuries, during the Song Dynasty.

cramped / kræmpt/
adj. not having enough space for the people in it

steeped /stiːpt/
adj. deeply surrounded or influenced by sth.

evanescent /ˌiːvəˈnesnt/
adj. disappearing quickly from sight or memory
tint /tɪnt/
v. to add a small amount of color to sth.

anonymous
/ə'nɒnıməs/
adj. without any
  unusual or
  interesting
  features

break the mould
  to change what
  people expect
  from a situation,
  especially by acting
  in a dramatic and
  original way

mediocrity
/ˌmiːdi'ɒkrəti/
n. the quality of being
  average or not very
  good

dissipation /ˌdɪsɪ'peɪʃn/
n. the process of
  disappearing or
  making sth.
  disappear

embellish /ɪm'belɪʃ/
v. to make sth. more
  beautiful by adding
  decorations to it

anonymous modern style. I wanted my complex to be more mysterious, and unlike typical modern architecture it is also inspired by nature. This was inevitably going to create a contrast, a conflict. The black and the sense of mystery served to **break the mould**, to distance myself from the **mediocrity** of the context.

5　*This project has been granted a Gold LEED[5] Certificate, one of the highest American standards for environmental sustainability in architecture. Where does your environmental intelligence lie?*

6　In reality it is a matter of qualities that all buildings ought to have today: natural ventilation, purification of the air inside, special glass that avoids the **dissipation** of energy, and harvesting of rainwater. In summer the air is cooled by passing under the pool of water that **embellishes** the plaza and is then channeled along the façades of the towers, to be distributed on each floor. But even more than these aspects I like to stress the experience generated by the architecture. For me the environmental sustainability of the design lies above all in the fluid forms with which we have created an "urban valley" that welcomes sunlight and nature. There is even a waterfall in the lobby of the towers.

7　*The risk of losing sight of nature is a real one in China. In addition to Beijing, with 21 million inhabitants, there are fifteen cities with a population*

5　LEED stands for Leadership in Energy and Environmental Design, is a green building rating program. It operates under the umbrella of the U.S. Green Building Council (USGBC), a non-profit coalition of building industry leaders. The goal of the rating system is to encourage and reward sustainable design across several metrics—sustainable site choice, energy savings, water efficiency, reduction of CO_2 emissions, and indoor environmental quality, among others—while improving company profitability and employee well-being.

of over 10 million. A few months ago, the government announced the establishment of Xiong'an, a macro region with over 100 million inhabitants around Beijing. Is sprawl the correct response to the massive urban migration under way?

8   What will extend around Beijing within a few years, taking the name of Xiong'an to the south and Jingjinji to the north, is just one of China's new urban constellations. Shanghai will **fuse** with Hangzhou and Suzhou. And then there's the so-called Pearl River Delta, the region comprising Zhuhai, Jiangmen and Zhongshan. While 70% of China's population lives in cities today, this will rise to 90%. So it is obvious that we are going to have to deal with density, but the challenge is to find the right way to construct. We mustn't copy America with its big buildings. Instead we need to go back to the tradition of the Chinese cities that draw inspiration from nature. Those same concepts and that philosophy should be applied on a grander scale than that of a (regular) contemporary megalopolis.

9   *In tackling this new and rapid phase of urbanization, has the government consulted you and other influential Chinese planners?*

10   On the urban planning front no, at least not so far. But the government has recently **commissioned** from us a social housing project of four thousand units in Beijing. Naturally these will be low-cost buildings, and yet we will be able to create a continuity with the landscape and a strong sense of community in this place. We will use very simple materials but there will be many gardens, collective spaces and balconies. Where nature is concerned there are no social classes.

fuse /fjuːz/
v. to be joined together to form a single thing

commission /kəˈmɪʃn/
v. to officially ask sb. to write, make or create sth. or to do a piece of work for you

panorama

/ˌpænəˈrɑːmə/

n. a description, study or set of pictures that presents all the different aspects or stages of a particular subject, event, etc.

tangible /ˈtændʒəbl/

adj. that can be clearly seen to exist; that you can touch or feel

affirm /əˈfɜːm/

v. to state clearly or publicly that sth. is true or that you support sth. strongly

11 *What will happen to the countryside and to farming in this new **panorama** of great sprawling metropolises?*

12 The idea is to concentrate on agriculture and make it an industry, something like what is already happening in the United States.

13 *At the Climate Change Conference in 2015 China showed that it had developed a greater environmental awareness. Are there **tangible** signs of this new attitude?*

14 In Beijing for example there has been a great deal of progress on the pollution front. In the last two years the government has taken drastic steps, like closing factories operating in the city, prohibiting the use of coal as a fuel for heating houses in the winter and even placing limits on the production of dust by the building trade. For cars the standards are stricter than those in Europe. They have to meet the requirements or they are not allowed on the road. And the results can already be seen. The quality of the air has improved greatly this year.

15 *You have worked all over the world. How would you describe the difference among architecture in Rome, in Los Angeles and in Beijing? In China everything is oversize. We count in millions; you count in tens of millions...*

16 Human feelings are the same on any scale, but when you design for large contexts a social and collective outlook comes more into play. In China our studio uses architecture as a means of **affirming** principles, of tackling conflicts, of stimulating debate on social themes. Here our architecture can be a voice that indicates new possibilities, and the conceptual debate becomes the true meaning of the project. In Los Angeles in a way anything is possible:

There we try to be critical because we don't like the commercial approach. We are for an emotional architecture that is close to nature. In Rome on the other hand, it is difficult and perhaps impossible to introduce innovation. But of the three cities, the one that has most history is Beijing.

(1,191 words)

Theme-Related Words & Expressions

megalopolis	特大都市
truss	桁架
condominium	公寓
interior	内饰
lot	（有某种用途的）一块地
complex	建筑群
ventilation	通风
façade	建筑物外立面
sprawl	（城市的）无计划扩张区域

Prepare/Probe

❶ Reading Comprehension

Answer the following questions according to the passage.

1) What is the purpose of this interview?

_____

_____

2) Why is Ma Yansong interviewed?

_____

_____

3) Why did the interviewer mention Batman's Gotham City? How can you analyze the interviewer's question here?

_____

_____

4) Do the interviewer and the interviewee have a similar judgement on the dealings of nature in and around Beijing? Why?

_____

_____

5) How is Beijing different from Rome and Los Angeles in terms of architecture in Ma Yansong's opinion?

_____

_____

Ⅱ Structure Building

Check your understanding of the overall structure of the passage by completing the following diagram.

Questions About Chaoyang Park Plaza	Answers
Exterior and design inspiration (Paras. 1–4)	• It is inspired by 1) _____. • It is also inspired by 2) _____. • It serves to create a(n) 3) _____ and break the 4) _____.
Environmental 5) _____ (Paras. 5–6)	• Common 6) _____: natural 7) _____, purification of the inside air, etc. • Unique experience: an "urban valley" in 8) _____ forms that 9) _____ sunlight and nature.
Questions About Urban Planning in Beijing	**Answers**
Massive urban 10) _____ (Paras. 7–12)	• A response to the 11) _____ problem. • The right way is to draw inspiration from 12) _____ and 13) _____.

Continued

14) _____ of environmental protection (Paras. 13–14)	• Drastic steps have been taken: 15) _____ _____ factories in the city; 16) _____ _____ coal used for heating fuel; 17) _____ strict standards on cars. • The result is the greatly 18) _____ ____ air quality.
19) _____ among several megalopolises (Paras. 15–16)	• Social and collective outlook comes more into play in larger 20) _____. • In Beijing, the architecture can be a(n) 21) _____; in Los Angeles, the architecture tends to be 22) _____ _____; in Rome, the architecture is difficult to be 23) _____.

Practice

❶ Vocabulary Practice

1. **Match the following theme-related words and expressions in Column A with their Chinese equivalents in Column B.**

   Column A

   1) tourist and cultural attraction

   2) printing works

   3) macro-region

   4) massive urban migration

   5) urban constellation

   6) opening

   7) well-lit

   8) anonymous modern style

   9) a strong sense of community

   10) rectangular lot

   11) natural landscape

   12) urban planning

   Column B

   A. 落成典礼

   B. 城市星群

   C. 无个性的现代风格

   D. 灯光明亮的

   E. 旅游文化名胜

   F. 自然景观

   G. 印刷厂

   H. 长方形用地

   I. 大规模城市迁移

   J. 大区

   K. 城市规划

   L. 强烈的社区意识

2. Group the words and expressions related to Beijing. You may find the words and expressions from Exercise 1 and the reading passage. Start with the examples given below.

Characteristics	history; _____
Inspiration	nature; _____
Urban planning	sprawl; _____
Environmental awareness	conserving water; _____

3. Fill in the blanks with the words or phrases in the box. Change the form if necessary.

on a grand scale	tangible	affirm	mediocrity	steep
break the mould	in any case	embellish	commission	fuse

1) Polluting _____, such as the use of coal for heating in winter, is no longer tolerated.

2) The two architectural firms have been _____ into a single one.

3) You can _____ them to design something especially for you.

4) _____ neither total reconstruction nor maintaining the status quo is effective to cure the urban diseases.

5) The local government _____ that the historical building would be relocated.

6) The downtown dwellers are rebelling at _____ price increases.

7) The revolutionary work did much to _____ of the old urban sociology.

8) His career started brilliantly, and then sank into _____.

9) There should be some _____ evidence that the community is starting to be revitalized.

10) The wall was _____ with carvings in red and blue.

❶ Sentence Practice

Study the sentence structure first, and then translate each of the given Chinese sentences into English by imitating the sentence structure.

1) The historic core of the Chinese capital <u>is destined to</u> become a tourist and cultural attraction at the center of this megalopolis <u>with</u> a population of over 100 million. (Para. 1)

   翻译：中国人民和发展中国家的人民注定会成为好朋友，因为他们有着相似的过往、目标和愿景。

   _____

   _____

2) <u>To the question about</u> who has a recipe for growth, he advises us to look for inspiration in nature and traditional architecture. (Para. 1)

   翻译：有关保持可持续增长的问题，改革开放不仅是在巨大的市场不确定性中的一个富有远见的选择，也是解决困扰全球增长的一些难题的良方。

   _____

   _____

3) This project <u>has been granted</u> a Gold LEED Certificate, one of the highest American standards for environmental sustainability in architecture. (Para. 5)

   翻译：中宣部授予云南省丽江市华坪女子高级中学校长张桂梅"时代楷模"称号，以表彰其为贫困家庭女孩教育所做的贡献。

   _____

   _____

4) <u>Where</u> nature <u>is concerned</u> there are no social classes. (Para. 10)

   翻译：涉及网络安全的问题，网络空间是数百万人共同的虚拟家园，一个纯净健康的在线环境符合所有用户的最佳利益。

   _____

   _____

5) In China our studio uses architecture <u>as a means of</u> affirming principles, <u>of</u> tackling conflicts, <u>of</u> stimulating debate on social themes. (Para. 16)

翻译：作为构建人类命运共同体的切实手段，"一带一路"倡议为世界带来了新的相互理解，激发了全球的想象力，并对国际交流贡献了新思想和新方法。

_____

_____

Ⅲ Discourse Practice

Complete the fragments with the suitable words or phrases in the box, and then sequence the fragments in the correct order. Change the form if necessary. You may not use any of the words or phrases more than once.

affirm	critical	stress	on the other hand
agreeable	instead	for	is concerned

A. "Architecture is not just an object that you place in the environment," Wang Shu explains. "Your experience of the architecture starts far away from the building. Architecture is not only the house in itself; it also includes a big area around it. All of this is architecture." Shu is not _____ to the limitations on the responsibility as an architect.

B. The couple is _____ a society that is good for people to live in. "Real culture starts from the ground," says Wang Shu. And he recounts his favorite project: designing a public toilet and washroom for a rural Chinese village which became a local gathering spot for all of the villagers.

C. His studio, Amateur Architecture Studio, co-founded together with Shu's wife Lu Wenyu, focuses on architecture that fosters community and works from the bottom up.

D. When society _____, Wang Shu _____, securing variety and local diversity is the real challenge in China as well as the Western world.

E. _____, modern societies have strong centralizing forces that level out differences, he states.

F. _____, he maintains "Architecture can change the life of people and give them a new right away. This is not a job for normal people to do. This should be the work of God."

G. The Chinese architect Wang Shu's buildings—a crossover between traditional Chinese culture and large-scale modern architecture—have earned him the prestigious Pritzker Prize. "Democracy means a really diverse society," he _____ in this inspiring interview.

H. Shu is _____ to the common understanding of Western democracy versus Chinese centralization.

Sequence: _____

Produce

Prepare and Rehearse an Interview with an Architect

🔢 Recap of the Previous Sessions

In Pretest, you've gained a basic understanding of Chinese architecture. In Prepare/Probe, you've grasped the main idea and structure of the text. In Practice, you've familiarized yourself with the necessary language points, sentence patterns, and the key information needed for Produce. Now it's time to consider the production of an interview.

🔢 Definition and Types of Interview

The word "interview" comes from Latin and middle French words meaning to "see between" or "see each other". Generally, an interview is a formal meeting between two people (the interviewer and the interviewee) where questions are asked by the interviewer to obtain information, qualities, attitudes, wishes, etc. from the interviewee. The person who answers the questions in an interview is called an interviewee. The person who asks the questions in an interview is called an interviewer.

There are many different types of interviews, and concerned with our production task, the following interviews can be considered:

- **Structured interviews**: Structured interviews tend to follow formal procedures; the interviewer follows a predetermined agenda or questions.
- **Unstructured interviews**: When the interview does not follow the formal rules or procedures, it is called an unstructured interview. The discussion

will probably be free-flowing and may shift rapidly from one subject to another depending on the interests of the interviewee and the interviewer.

- **Semi-structured interviews**: Conducted conversationally with one interviewee at a time, it employs a blend of closed- and open-ended questions, often accompanied by follow-up why or how questions. The dialogue can meander around the topics on the agenda—rather than adhering slavishly to verbatim questions as in a structured interview—and may delve into totally unforeseen issues. They are relaxing, engaging, in-person and could last longer than structured interviews, although they may not last as long as entirely unstructured ones. About one hour is considered a reasonable maximum length in order to minimize fatigue for both the interviewer and the interviewee.

- **Informal or conversational interview**: In the conversational interview, no predetermined questions are asked, in order to remain as open and adaptable as possible to the interviewee's nature and priorities; during the interview the interviewer "goes with the flow".

Ⅲ Communicative Techniques

1. Interview preparation

The following guidelines and tips are helpful for preparing an interview:

1) Determine the type of the interview

Consider the purpose of the interview. Is it for a research, a public occasion or for an investigation? As this interview will take place in a public setting with audiences involved, the interviewer needs to think about which type of interview is best for the audiences from different backgrounds and age groups.

2) Determine the structure of the interview

Consider the length and relationship between you and your interviewee. Within a scheduled ceremony, the time for the interview is probably limited, but not too short to miss any important messages, and in this chapter's production task, though the higher social status and the seniority of the interviewee suggest a relatively formal dialogue, your identity being a student interviewer and the connection between you—similar educational and professional background—indicate there is room for a relaxing conversation.

3) Review the necessary paperwork and plan questions

Research the person you are to interview, such as reading his/her personal webpage, social media, getting information about his/her recent project and major achievements. It's also important to search for his/her passions and interests. Reach out to the interviewee by messaging or emailing him/her with a brief self-introduction and a general interview outline.

4) Rehearse for the interview

You may practice with your partner and take turns to act as the interviewer and the interviewee. You may also proofread your questions and be prepared to dress up properly for the occasion.

5) Plan an appropriate environment in which to conduct the interview

You may watch other interviews of similar subjects, or famous or effective interviews with interviewees of similar backgrounds, and consider asking similar or different questions, learning from the interviewer's tone and body language, etc.

6) Be aware of body language

Nonverbal communication is important. When you're meeting people during the interview, remember the attributes you want your body language to display.

The following are some helpful preparation tips from successful interviewers.

1) Make your interviewee feel heard

Oprah Winfrey holds the record for most-viewed television interview (her interview with Michael Jackson) and she interviewed tens of thousands of people over the course of her career. Winfrey realized that every issue or problem that was featured on her show, at its root, was due to someone not being noticed or heard.

You may not be interviewing presidents or pop stars, but the principle still applies. Asking questions about the challenges facing your audience, and listening to their responses can provide valuable insights.

2) Don't be afraid to interrupt

Malcolm Gladwell is the author of five *New York Times* bestsellers. In Malcolm's master class he discusses how people tend to be afraid to interrupt. As an interviewer, one tactic Malcolm uses is to slow the interview with polite interruptions in an effort to get as much context and definition from his subject as possible. Asking clarifying questions is better than making assumptions about what your subject is saying.

3) Don't over-prepare

Larry King was dubbed "the most remarkable talk show host on TV ever" by *TV Guide* and "Master of the mic" by *Time Magazine*. To Larry, every interview was an exercise in curiosity. In a 2017 interview, Larry advocated for not having any agenda or preset list of questions. From Larry's perspective, the strategy of having a preset list of questions and objectives is in direct conflict to curious interviewing.

2. Conducting an interview

1) Start with greeting

If the interviewee comes to you, thank him/her for coming and meeting with you. However, if you come to the interviewee, just thank him/her for meeting with you. You can then either ask, "How's your day going?" or say, "I hope your day is going well." The idea is to make the interviewee feel welcomed and show your appreciation.

2) Phrase questions

To start the conversation, after you've greeted the interviewee, use some of the pre-prepared questions you wrote. Once he/she responds, ask natural follow-up questions, even if you haven't already written them down. Natural follow-up questions will make the interview seem more like a conversation.

Once the interviewee starts to talk, listen and do not interrupt or show no response. You can show your genuine interest and respect by nodding or giving short comment without cutting him/her off. Between different topics, use natural descriptions to transit to a new topic.

3) Adopt an investigative mindset

At this point in the process, you're prepared for the interview and ready to ask questions. It's important to make sure you adopt a mindset to examine the information your interviewee is giving you. Focusing on uncovering the unknown and learning more about it can help lead your interview in a valuable direction.

4) Follow up for more detail

Sometimes all it takes is a small phrase to get to the detail you're really searching for. It can be hard to think of a follow-up prompt in the moment. Here are a few examples:

• Tell me more...

• Expand on...

• What did you mean by...

• Could you describe...

Pick one of these that feels most organic to you, write it down, and reference it during your interview.

5) Take advice from a 3-year-old

If those prompts don't reveal the information you're looking for, consider asking "Why?" multiple times. This method, popular with many 3-year-olds, was developed at Toyota Motor Company and was instrumental in helping them develop their continuous improvement approach to manufacturing. While it might seem clumsy, asking "Why?" multiple times can lead the conversation toward a path of discovering the root cause of an issue.

6) Leave some room

Once you've asked all the questions on your list, make time for the interviewee to cover any ground they think is important that perhaps you missed. While many interviewees might not offer this information up, try prompting them with one of these examples:

• Is there anything you want to add?

• Is there anything you want to discuss that we didn't cover?

• What didn't I ask that you want to talk about?

The following are some basic principles of don'ts and do's for normal interviews:

The Don'ts

• Avoid Yes/No questions

Yes/No questions lead to Yes/No answers which are short, with virtually no rich description. For example:

Original Yes/No questions:

Interviewer: Is your married life the same here as it would be back at home?

[Yes]

Interviewer: Have you changed in any ways since coming here?

[No]

Improved Version 1:

Interviewer: What was your married life like back in Australia?

Interviewer: How is your married life organized now?

Improved Version 2:

Interviewer: Now I would like to ask a few questions about your married life back in Sri Lanka. First, can you tell me how you divide the daily work?

• Avoid multiple-choice and double-barreled questions

Here is an example: "Why did you come to Canada? Was it for the climate or for work or to reunite with a family member?" By phrasing questions in multiple-choice format, the interviewer obliges the interviewee to select an answer from the provided choices.

• Don't switch topics too frequently

Consider: How many topics did the interview with Ma Yansong cover?

• Avoid leading questions

A leading question is a type of question that implies or contains its own answer. By contrast, a neutral question is expressed in a way that doesn't suggest its own answer.

Consider: Are there any leading questions in the interview with Ma Yansong?

The Do's

• Listen attentively.

• Ask about sensitive issues skillfully.

• Adjust questions to the interviewee's situation.

• Ask for clarification.

• Ask open-ended questions.

3. **Ending an interview**

An easy way to end an interview with a celebrity is to say something along the lines of, "Unfortunately that's all the time we have. It was such a pleasure talking to you. Thanks for making the time." Try to show your appreciation and don't run over the time limit. As a formal thank-you gesture, you can send him/her an email at the end of the day, or a nice thank-you gift when the interview comes to an end.

Post-Learning Evaluation

No.	Statements	Strongly agree	Agree	Not sure	Disagree	Strongly disagree
1	I have grasped the words related to the theme.					
2	I am familiar with the key words and phrases in the passage.					
3	I am familiar with the major points of the passage.					
4	I am familiar with the terms explained in the footnotes.					
5	I am familiar with the major types of interviews.					
6	I am able to apply certain helpful expressions in conducting an interview.					
7	I know how to make effective questions in interviews.					
8	I am able to prepare and give an interview when assigned to.					
9	I can detect and analyze the leading questions when being interviewed.					

Continued

No.	statements	Strongly agree	Agree	Not sure	Disagree	Strongly disagree
10	I am able to introduce something about urban planning in Beijing in my own way when being interviewed in English.					
11	I understand my role either as an interviewer or interviewee, and I have improved my teamwork skills through peer interaction.					
12	I know how to analyze more critically towards the Western coverage on Chinese architecture.					
13	As a Chinese citizen, I have a better understanding of Chinese city development problems, solutions and future possibilities.					
14	I am proud that Beijing is a megalopolis that combines rapid modernization and profound history.					
15	I am aware of the differences of the urbanization concept between the West and the East.					
16	I am willing to share my view to clear any misunderstandings in international communication on the subject of Chinese architecture.					
17	After learning this chapter, I will tell stories on Chinese architecture to international friends when I have the opportunity.					

Chapter 7

China's Network Influentials

Pretest

How much do you know about the Internet celebrities or KOLs (Key Opinion Leaders, who are usually field experts or popular Internet users that have developed massive digital audiences) in China? Can you match some terms about KOLs with their proper explanations?

1) a marketing strategy whose purpose is to use one or multiple celebrities to advertise a specific product or service

2) the quick sell out of newly-advertised goods; usually the transaction is made in seconds

3) an approach to the management of information that treats human attention as a scarce commodity and applies economic theory to solve various information management problems

4) the platform for broadcasting or receiving live video and sound of an event over the Internet

5) independently operated accounts run by individual users posting self-produced content on social media platforms, such as WeChat and Weibo

6) the fusion of live streaming videos and e-commerce; selling a featured product using live video streaming so as to get high return on investment

7) a popular function in many live streaming platforms where viewers can give streamers tips or virtual gifts

8) celebrities, social media icons or anyone with over 1 million followers

( ) A. live streaming platform

( ) B. attention economy

( ) C. self-media

( ) D. live commerce

( ) E. celebrity endorsement

( ) F. mega influencer

( ) G. seckill

( ) H. reward function

Pretask

You are a student journalist of *The Heights*, the campus newspaper of ABC University which not only covers campus events and school news, but also delves into technology, social media, and Internet culture issues that reflect the interest of students. Due to students' strong interest in Internet celebrities in China and influencer economy, the editor assigns you to cover the news on one of the top influencers in China. Please try to gather information from different sources, determine what is truthful and what is valuable, and then present the news article in a certain light or angle.

1) To accomplish the task, I plan to take the following steps:

_____.

For the first step, I think _____
might be challenging.

For the second step, I think _____
might be challenging.

_____

_____

2) I expect to achieve the following goals after learning the unit:

_____

_____

Passage

Country Life: The Young Female Farmer Who Is Now a Top Influencer in China

This article is adapted from Adrienne Matei's article from The Guardian[1] *(January, 2020). It provides a balanced perspective on the Chinese country-life vlogger Li Ziqi. The author goes beyond the facts on the surface and gives an analysis of Li's popularity through interviews with people concerned and research into background information.*

garner /ˈgɑːnə(r)/
v. to obtain or collect sth. such as information, support, etc.
idyllic /ɪˈdɪlɪk/
adj. peaceful and beautiful; perfect, without problems
rustic /ˈrʌstɪk/
adj. simple, old-fashioned, and not spoiled by modern developments, in a way that is typical of the countryside
chic /ʃiːk/
n. the quality of being fashionable and attractive

1   Li Ziqi, 29, has **garnered** millions of followers with her videos of her **idyllic** life in rural Sichuan. Is she too good to be true?

2   Since she began posting **rustic-chic** videos of her life in rural Sichuan Province in 2016, Li Ziqi, 29, has become one of China's biggest social media stars. She has 22 million followers on the microblogging site Weibo, 34 million on Douyin and another 8.3 million on YouTube (Li has been active on YouTube for the last two years).

3   Li's videos, which she initially produced by herself and now makes with a small team, emphasize

---

1   *The Guardian* is an influential daily newspaper published in London, generally considered one of the United Kingdom's leading newspapers. It is rated Left-Center biased based on story selection that moderately favors the Left and Mixed for factual reporting.

beautiful countryside and ancient tradition. In videos **soundtracked** by **tranquil** flute music, Li crafts her own furniture out of bamboo and dyes her clothing with fruit skins. If she wants soy sauce, she grows the soybeans herself; a video about making an egg yolk dish starts with her hatching ducklings. The meals she creates are often elaborate demonstrations of how many delicious things can be done with a particular seasonal ingredient like ginger or green plums.

4   There is even a Li Ziqi online shop, where fans can purchase versions of the steel "chopper" knife she uses to dice the vegetables she plucks from her plentiful garden, or **replicas** of the old-fashioned shirts she wears while **foraging** for wild mushrooms and magnolia blossoms in the misty mountainside.

5   While she occasionally reveals a behind-the-scenes peek at her process, Li, who did not respond to interview requests for this article, is very private. **By all accounts**, she struggled to find steady work in a city before returning to the countryside to care for her **ailing** grandmother (who appears in her videos).

6   Recently, Li has been thrust into a wider **spotlight** as an example of how to promote Chinese culture for a younger, more social media-savvy generation. In 2018, she was selected as the "good young netizen" and role model for Chinese youth. In September 2019, *People's Daily* gave Li their "People's Choice" award, while last month, state media praised Li for helping to promote traditional culture globally, and the Communist Youth League named her an ambassador of a program promoting the economic **empowerment** of rural youth.

7   As the government increasingly **champions** her, Chinese citizens have taken to Weibo to question

soundtrack
/'saʊndtræk/
v. to provide (a movie) with the recorded music
tranquil /'træŋkwɪl/
adj. quiet and peaceful

replica /'replɪkə/
n. a very good or exact copy of sth.
forage /'fɒrɪdʒ/
v. to search widely for food

by all accounts according to what other people say
ailing /'eɪlɪŋ/
adj. ill and not likely to get better
spotlight /'spɒtlaɪt/
n. attention from newspapers, television and the public
empowerment /ɪm'paʊəmənt/
n. the act of giving sb. more control over his/her own life or the situation he/she is in
champion /'tʃæmpiən/
v. to fight for or speak in support of a group of people or a belief

whether Li's polished, rather one-dimensional portrayal of farm work conveys anything truly meaningful about contemporary China, especially to her growing international audience on YouTube.

8   They have a point: Li's videos reveal as much about the day-to-day labor of most Chinese farmers as the *Martha Stewart Show*[2] does about the American working class. As Li Bochun, director of Beijing-based Chinese Culture **Rejuvenation** Research Institute told the media last month: "The traditional lifestyle Li Ziqi presents in her videos is…not widely followed." Dr. Dong Yikun from Beijing Foreign Studies University also added that what Li shows in her videos does not represent how the majority of rural residents live their lives.

9   However, that's not to say the beautiful forests and compelling traditions of Li's videos are not genuine; like many social media creators, she simply focuses on the most charming elements of a bigger picture.

10   So what do Li's videos reflect about modern China, if not average daily life in the countryside?

11   For one, they say something about the **mindset** of her audience—primarily urban millennials, for whom a traditional culture craze known as "fugu" or "hanfu" has been an **aesthetic** trend for a number of years.

12   "Fugu", according to Yang Chunmei, professor of Chinese history and philosophy at Qufu Normal

rejuvenation
/rɪˌdʒuːvəˈneɪʃn/
n. the act of making sth. work much better or become much better again

mindset /ˈmaɪndset/
n. a set of attitudes or fixed ideas that sb. has and that are often difficult to change
aesthetic /iːsˈθetɪk/
adj. connected with beauty and the study of beauty

---

2 Martha Stewart is an American retail businesswoman, writer, television personality, and former model. The *Martha Stewart Show* is one of America's most cherished weekday talk shows. The show, which was hosted by Martha Stewart, provides television viewers and audience members with tips on cooking, craft-making, gardening, and interior design.

University, reflects the "**romanticized pastoral**" desires of youth "disillusioned by today's everchanging, industrial, consumerist society." In practice, it looks like young people integrating more traditional clothing into their daily looks, watching historical dramas and following rural lifestyle **influencers** like Li. (While Li is an extremely popular example of the trend, she's not the only young farmer vlogging in China right now, and outdoor cooking videos of people making meals with wild ingredients and scant equipment are a genre of their own on Douyin.)

13   Also at play in Li's popularity is the particular tenor of Chinese **wistfulness**. "It's called *Xiangchou*. *Xiang* means the countryside or rural life, and *chou* means to long for it, to miss it," says Linda Qian, an Oxford University PhD candidate studying **nostalgia**'s role in the **revitalization** of China's villages.

14   "It is quite prevalent for youth living the city life. They get really sick of [the city] so the countryside"— or a fantasy of it—"looks increasingly like the ideal image of what a good life should be."

15   Qian also likens Li's appeal to that of *Man vs Wild*[3]-style entertainment in the West. "We've gotten to a certain point of materialism and consumption where there's only so much you can buy, and we're like, 'What other experiences can I have?'" she says. "So we go back to what humans can do."

16   In addition to portraying an idyllic rural lifestyle in China, Li embodies a kind of rural success the government hopes to generate more of through recent **initiatives**. With the aim of **alleviating** rural

---

3   *Man vs Wild* is a Discovery Channel show in which famed survivalist Bear Grylls runs the audience through techniques and strategies to keep oneself alive when lost and lonely in the wilderness.

romanticize /rəʊ'mæntɪsaɪz/
v. to make sth. seem more attractive or interesting than it really is

pastoral /'pɑːstərəl/
adj. showing country life or the countryside, especially in a romantic way

influencer /'ɪnfluənsə(r)/
n. a person or thing that influences sb./sth., especially a person with the ability to influence potential buyers of a product or service by recommending it on social media

wistfulness /'wɪstflnəs/
n. a slightly sad feeling caused by thinking about sth. that you would like to have, especially sth. in the past that you can no longer have

nostalgia /nɒ'stældʒə/
n. a sad feeling mixed with pleasure when you think of happy times in the past

revitalization /ˌriːˌvaɪtəlaɪ'zeɪʃn/
n. the process of making sth. stronger, more active or more healthy

initiative /ɪ'nɪʃətɪv/
n. a new plan for dealing with a particular problem or for achieving a particular purpose

alleviate /ə'liːvieɪt/
v. to make sth. less severe

poverty, the Communist Youth League has embarked on an effort to send more than 10 million urban youth to "rural zones" by 2022, in order to "increase their skills, spread civilization, and promote science and technology".

17 "We need young people to use science and technology to help the countryside innovate its traditional development models," Zhang Linbin, deputy head of a township in central Hunan Province, told the *Global Times*[4] last April.

18 By using technology to create her own rural economic opportunities while **simultaneously** championing forms of traditional Chinese culture before a huge audience, Li may seem like a Chinese dream that has come true.

19 According to Professor Ka-Ming Wu, a cultural **anthropologist** at the Chinese University of Hong Kong, "Li represents a new wave of Chinese soft power in that she's so creative and aesthetically good, and knows how to appeal to a general audience whether they're Chinese or not." In fact, she has generated genuine domestic, and especially international interest in rural Chinese traditions than any initiative of the past decade.

20 Maryland Smith's Professor Amna Kirmani frames the Li Ziqi phenomenon differently. "Her videos reflect a high level of **authenticity** and come off as **awe** inspiring," says Kirmani. "These are key ingredients for tapping into an influencer economy that is growing very strongly in China and worldwide. And it's far from hitting its peak."

simultaneously
/ˌsɪml'teiniəsli/
adv. at the same time as sth. else

anthropologist
/ˌænθrə'pɒlədʒɪst/
n. a person who studies the human race, especially its origins, development, customs and beliefs

authenticity
/ˌɔːθen'tɪsəti/
n. the quality of being real or true
awe /ɔː/
n. a feeling of great respect and liking for sb./sth.

---

4 *Global Times* is an English-language Chinese newspaper under *People's Daily*. It comments on international issues from a nationalistic perspective.

21 In regard to cultural stereotyping, "Li Ziqi, if anything, is countering an American-held **stereotype** of China in terms of the 'Made in China' catchphrase including the negative **connotation** of cheap labor that's producing goods and exports," Kirmani says. "In this way, she is improving Americans' perception of China."

22 However you feel about Li as a cultural force, her ability to flourish despite a unique set of contradictory circumstances is impressive. Will other YouTube influencers become successful following Li Ziqi's path? **Algorithms** might suggest yes. Aside from help via technology and algorithms, brand recognition and the influencers' personal **charisma** are very hard to duplicate. It will prove very difficult for another to copy Li Ziqi's **serene** and **minimalist** content.

(1,303 words)

stereotype /ˈsteriətaɪp/
n. a belief or idea of what a particular type of person or thing is like

connotation /ˌkɒnəˈteɪʃn/
n. a quality or an idea that a word makes you think of that is more than its basic meaning

algorithm /ˈælgərɪðəm/
n. a set of rules that must be followed when solving a particular problem

charisma /kəˈrɪzmə/
n. a natural ability to attract and interest other people and make them admire you

serene /səˈriːn/
adj. very calm or peaceful

minimalist /ˈmɪnɪməlɪst/
adj. (of art, music or design) using very simple ideas or a very small number of simple elements

Theme-Related Words & Expressions

idyllic life	田园诗般的生活
post videos	发布视频
social media star	社交媒体明星；网红
microblogging site	微博网站
ancient tradition	传统民俗

old-fashioned shirt	复古风格的衣着
be thrust into spotlight	被推到聚光灯下
state media	官方媒体
promote traditional culture globally	向全世界推广传统文化
Chinese Culture Rejuvenation	中华文化复兴
social media creator	社交媒体创作者
traditional culture craze	传统文化热潮
urban millennial	都市千禧一代
aesthetic trend	审美趋势
vlog	视频播客
wild ingredient	野生食材
revitalization of China's villages	中国乡村振兴
alleviate rural poverty	缓解农村贫困
soft power	软实力
tap into an influencer economy	开发网红经济
cultural stereotyping	文化刻板印象
catchphrase	流行语；热词
cultural force	文化力量
brand recognition	品牌认知度

Prepare/Probe

❶ Reading Comprehension

Answer the following questions according to the passage.

1) Why do some Chinese citizens question whether Li's work "conveys anything truly meaningful about contemporary China"?

_____

_____

2) Why do Li's videos appeal to urban millennials who love old customs and traditions?

_____

_____

3) Why does the author mention *Xiangchou* in the analysis of Li's popularity?

_____

_____

4) What are the reasons behind the Chinese government's recognition of Li Ziqi's contribution to the promotion of Chinese culture?

_____

_____

5) Why is it difficult for other influencers to copy Li Ziqi's success?

_____

_____

Ⅱ Structure Building

Check your understanding of the overall structure of the passage by completing the following diagram.

Lead (Para. 1)
Li Ziqi, 29, has garnered millions of followers with her videos of her idyllic life in rural Sichuan. Is she too good to be true?

Facts (Paras. 2–7)	**Quotes** (Paras. 8–21)
1. Li's popularity	1. Quotes from professors or scholars
• Her followers;	• Director of Beijing-based Chinese Culture Rejuvenation Research Institute: "The traditional lifestyle Li Ziqi presents in her videos is not widely 6) _____."
• Her videos;	
• Her online shop.	
2. Government & state media's attitudes	
• Thrust her into spotlight;	• Professor of Chinese history and philosophy at Qufu Normal University: "Fugu" reflects the
• Praised her for helping to promote 1) _____ globally;	

Continued

• Named her a(n) 2) _____ of a program promoting the economic empowerment of rural youth. 3. Chinese citizens' attitudes to Li • Question whether her videos convey 3) _____ .	"romanticized pastoral desires of youth". • An Oxford University PhD candidate: "It (*Xiangchou*) is quite prevalent for youth living the city life."
Author's analyses (Paras. 10–18) 1. Li's videos reveal the 4) _____ _____ of urban millennials: "fugu" and Chinese wistfulness (nostalgia or *Xiangchou*). 2. Li embodies the rural 5) _____ the government hopes to generate.	• A cultural anthropologist at the Chinese University of Hong Kong: "Li represents a new wave of 7) _____ " • Maryland Smith's Professor: "She is improving 8) _____ _____ ."
Scholars' analyses (Paras. 19–21) 1. Li has generated genuine domestic and international interest in rural Chinese traditions. 2. Li changed an American-held stereotype of China.	2. Quotes from officials • A deputy head of a township: "We need young people to use science and technology to help the countryside 9) _____ _____ its traditional development models."

Concluding statement (Para. 22)

However you feel about Li as a cultural force, her ability to flourish is impressive. It will prove very difficult for another to 10) _____ .

Practice

❶ Vocabulary Practice

1. **Match the words in Column A with those in Column B to form appropriate collocations.**

Column A	Column B
1) garner	A. videos/photos/ads/responses/links/ comments
2) post	B. demonstration/production/design
3) craft	C. interest/ideas/profits/revenue/wealth

4) embody	D. followers/views/likes
5) generate	E. award/title
6) give/present/win/earn	F. furniture/toys/projects
7) elaborate	G. success/principle/ideal/value/truth/spirit
8) top/biggest/beauty/food/travel/country-life	H. influencer/ Internet celebrity / social media star / blogger/vlogger

2. **Fill in the blanks using the appropriate collocations formed in Exercise 1. Change the form if necessary.**

1) 28-year-old Li Jiaqi rose from being a shop assistant at a cosmetics store to become China's top beauty _____. With over 80 million followers across social media, Li has created an online empire that _____ more revenue than many shopping malls and listed companies.

2) Li Ziqi is a food and _____ blogger and Internet celebrity. She activated her YouTube channel on August 22, 2017, and posted her first _____ "Making a dress with grape skins, what kind of experience is it?" two days later, which has _____ more than 20.4 million views so far.

3) Wang Dewen, also known as Grandpa Amu, became an influencer by _____ toys for his grandson. Grandpa Amu's fine workmanship and _____ design has won the hearts of 700,000 YouTube subscribers.

4) Viya has won the _____ of "Alibaba's 2019 Anchor for Poverty Alleviation" because of her charity work. She livestreams for farmers in rural areas in China, helping them to promote their goods.

3. **Fill in the blanks with the words or phrases in the box. Change the form if necessary.**

spotlight	ambassador	integrate	appeal	by all accounts
flourish	promote	embark	initiative	demonstration

1) Li Ziqi, the popular vlogger whose videos focus on the beautiful scenery and the rural life in the Chinese countryside, is now seen as a cultural _____ for the country.

2) Her videos have little words or conversations, yet they _____ to international audience. Without a word commending China, Li tells a good Chinese story.

3) An influencer _____ a brand's product and gets a commission based on sales through the influencer's platform.

4) Now that influencer marketing has become mainstream, some new influencers are thrust into the _____ by posting videos on TikTok, YouTube, Twitter or Facebook.

5) In an anti-poverty _____, 1.88 million poor residents in Guizhou Province were moved out of environmentally-vulnerable mountainous regions.

6) Intangible cultural heritage must be thoughtfully managed if it is to _____ in an increasingly globalized world.

7) 91% of 18-to-34-year-old consumers seek out trusted influencers and follow their every move. Influencer marketing is a clear _____ of attracting and establishing trust with these consumers.

8) Many brands have started _____ influencers into their social media marketing campaign to expand the reach of their message.

9) _____, Martha Stewart's *Homekeeping Handbook* is a pretty and practical package for everyone.

10) She _____ on a second career as a livestreamer on Alibaba's e-commerce platform Taobao selling beauty products.

❚❚ Sentence Practice

Study the sentence structure first, and then translate each of the given Chinese sentences into English by imitating the sentence structure.

1) <u>With the aim of</u> alleviating rural poverty, the Communist Youth League <u>has embarked on an effort to</u> send more than 10 million urban youth to "rural zones" by 2022, <u>in order to</u> "increase their skills, spread civilization, and promote science and technology". (Para. 16)

翻译：为了推动构建人类命运共同体，中国全面开展抗击新冠肺炎疫情国际合作，以确保疫苗公平分配，加快推进接种速度，弥合国际"免疫鸿沟"。

_____

2) <u>By</u> using technology to create her own rural economic opportunities <u>while</u> simultaneously championing forms of traditional Chinese culture

before a huge audience, Li may <u>seem like</u> a Chinese dream come true. (Para. 18)

翻译：通过推广普及冰雪运动，同时加快建设冰雪设施，全民健身活动似乎成为了冰雪产业发展的催化剂。

3) <u>According to</u> Professor Ka-Ming Wu, a cultural anthropologist at the Chinese University of Hong Kong, "Li represents a new wave of Chinese soft power <u>in that</u> she's so creative and aesthetically good..." (Para. 19)

翻译：英国 48 家集团俱乐部荣誉主席斯蒂芬·佩里说："从长远来看，全球化和多边贸易形式是不可阻挡的，因为他们是让人们满足需求、获得更好更安全环境的唯一途径。"

4) <u>In regard to</u> cultural stereotyping, "Li Ziqi, if anything, is countering an American-held stereotype of China <u>in terms of</u> the 'Made in China' catchphrase including the negative connotation of cheap labor that's producing goods and exports," Kirmani says. (Para. 21)

翻译：在可持续发展方面，从碳排放强度、能源利用率和能源安全来说，新能源汽车拥有诸多优势。

5) <u>However you feel about</u> Li as a cultural force, her <u>ability to</u> flourish despite a unique set of contradictory circumstances <u>is impressive</u>. (Para. 22)

翻译：不论你对中国的经济实力有什么看法，中国打赢人类历史上规模最大的脱贫攻坚战的能力令人赞叹。

Ⅲ Discourse Practice

Complete the news article about influencer marketing with suitable sentences in the box.

> A. Today, some brands recruit mega-influencers or macro-influencers for their B2B online marketing campaigns. Influencer marketing has helped businesses of all kinds build brand awareness, prolong engagement and generate sales.
>
> B. Without doubt, the influencer economy is changing.
>
> C. It was when they were sold out in a single day that she realized the power of the influencer economy, Penchansky recalled, speaking on a panel on Tuesday at Target's design studio in Chelsea.
>
> D. Beyond creating content for brands, another driving force of the influencer economy is the consumers' hunger for representation.

About a decade ago, Raina Penchansky, then vice president of communications at Coach, oversaw a campaign involving a collection of handbags designed by fashion bloggers. 1) _____

_____.

In 2010, Penchansky co-founded Digital Brand Architects, an agency that matches bloggers and social media persons with sponsors, a market that by 2017 had swelled to $1 billion on Instagram alone, according to Mediakix, another marketing agency.

2) _____.

The ecosystem is still expanding, extending beyond the biggest names, with even "micro-influencers" targeted by brands for their often devoted followers. According to fashion blogger Bryan Gambao, also known as Bryanboy, his more-than 600,000 Instagram followers make him a micro-influencer compared with celebrities with millions of fans.

"Early on for brands, it was about how we translate our influence into sales," Mason said. "Now when I'm working with brands, it's not to sell products. It's to change their way of approaching a customer or product." In other words, influencers are no longer just peddling products directly from brands to their followers. They're creating campaigns around a brand for a company and even building their own brands, as Mason did.

What matters, ultimately, is the credibility of the relationship between the brand or product and the influencer. The extent of his personal experience with brand partners, he said, "goes on from posting a picture on Instagram of me holding a bag, to me creating a video of events around the world that they send me to. All of this creates an image of me integrating with these brands on a 360 level."

3) _____ .

"We're living in this era of inclusivity where diversity—and authentic diversity—is so important," Mason said. "Brands and marketers need to say, 'We need to reflect the world around us regardless of what the data is showing us.'"

Penchansky said that's one reason why brands are so eager to work with influencers. "It's a huge reason why the influencer space took off in the first place," she said. "People are saying, 'I want to see people who look like me.' If you ignore that, it's counterintuitive to the space itself."

"With what's coming with Gen-Z and YouTube, we haven't even seen the capacity of influencers being able to generate revenue," she said.

4) _____ .

For brands wanting to continue to harness influencers' power, fresh challenges must be addressed. But make no mistake, new opportunities await those that understand and respond to the market's shifting dynamics.

Produce

Write a News Article About an Influencer in China

❶ Recap of the Previous Sessions

In Pretest, you've gained a basic understanding of Chinese KOLs. In Prepare/Probe, you've grasped the main idea and structure of the text. In Practice, you've familiarized yourself with the necessary language points, sentence patterns, and key information needed for Produce. Now it's time to consider the production of a news article about an influencer that you are interested in.

Ⅱ Definition of a News Article

A news article is a news report of any length, usually presented in a straightforward style and without editorial comment. It is a blend of a news article with a bit of interpretation of the facts without giving an opinion as to what the solution should be.

A good news article is concise, objective, complete (all key points) and original (in your own words).

Ⅲ Techniques of Writing a News Article

1. **Choose a newsworthy topic or event**

Step 1: Choose a top influencer who interests readers.

Think about why the story about the influencer is important, what readers already know, and why they care about the story you plan to write.

Step 2: Do research.

Use encyclopedias, Internet and other reference materials to get the facts you need, such as the background information, statistics, content production on social media platforms, people's comments, etc.

Step 3: Interview.

Think about who you would interview. Prepare interview questions and record answers.

2. **Write a strong lead**

1) Definition of a lead

A lead is the opening sentences of a piece of news or the first paragraph or two of a longer article in journalism. A lead must convey essential information, set the tone and attract people to continue reading.

2) Steps of writing a lead

Step 1: Summarize the main points of the story.

Step 2: Use the 5Ws and H rule. Decide which aspect of the story—who, what, when, where, why, how—is the most important. Put your most crucial information at the very beginning of the sentence. Important secondary information can go in subsequent sentences.

Step 3: Keep it short and to the point. Write first sentences of between 25 and 35 words, and no more than 40.

Step 4: Write in active voice. Avoid passive constructions.

For example:

- Two Hamilton County Commissioners plan to force the county's top administrator out of office today. (Summary lead)

- From Dan Ralescu's sun-warmed beach chair in Thailand, the Indian Ocean began to look oddly, not so much like waves but bread dough. (Anecdotal lead)

- What's increasing faster than the price of gasoline? Apparently, the cost of court lobbyists. (Question lead)

3. **Include quotes**

   Try to quote people to add accuracy and to add "at the scene" feeling. Place your quotes and be sure to identify key people in the story by their full name, occupation, and age.

For example:

- A student from ACVI, Ellie Markham, added, "This was such an inspiring event! I am so motivated!"

- "It is a load of rubbish," said Mr. Peter Kuman, vice president of the Retail Traders Association and its regional representative on the PNG Chamber of Commerce.

Ⅳ Organization of a news article

A typical news article is broken down into the headline, the lead, the body of the story and the conclusion.

Remember, in news writing, always use the inverted pyramid style, that is, place the most important facts at the start of the article and close with the least compelling elements. Ideally, the first paragraph should contain enough information to give the reader a good overview of the entire story. The rest of the article explains and expands on the beginning. A news article is roughly divided into the following four parts.

Headline	Choose a limited number of words to convey the main point of the news article.
Lead	In two or three sentences, write the basic facts by answering five important questions: Who did the thing of interest? What did they do? Where did they do it? When did they do it? Why did they do it?
Body	• Expand your basic facts to include several supporting details. • Continue to explain why the event happened and offer all the detail about how it came to take place. • Include quotes from different sources where appropriate. • Remember to write in third person (no "I/me" or "we/us") unless you are giving a direct quotation.
Conclusion	Write a very short paragraph that wraps up the news report, or finish with a section of additional related information which is still helpful to fully understand the context of the story.

Post-Learning Evaluation

No.	Statements	Strongly agree	Agree	Not sure	Disagree	Strongly disagree
1	I have grasped the expressions related to the theme.					
2	I am familiar with the key words and phrases in the passage.					
3	I am familiar with the major points of the passage.					
4	I am familiar with the terms explained in the footnotes.					
5	I am familiar with the organization of a news report or a news article.					
6	I am familiar with the skills of writing a lead and including quotes.					

Continued

No.	Statements	Strongly agree	Agree	Not sure	Disagree	Strongly disagree
7	I am familiar with the inverted pyramid style of news articles and steps of writing a news article.					
8	I am able to write a fact-based news article using third person narration when assigned to.					
9	I have a better understanding of China's Internet celebrities and influencer economy.					
10	I have a better understanding of the impact of Internet celebrities and influencer economy on our daily life.					
11	I take pride in the fact that Chinese influencer economy is growing rapidly and some influencers help promote Chinese culture to the world.					
12	I would form a more critical view towards the Western coverage on Chinese KOLs, and if there are some misunderstandings, I would like to explain.					
13	I understand my role in the accomplishment of the project, and I have improved my teamwork skills by collaborating with my team members through peer interaction.					
14	After learning this chapter, I will tell stories about Chinese KOLs or influencer economy to international friends when I have the opportunity.					

Continued

No.	Statements	Strongly agree	Agree	Not sure	Disagree	Strongly disagree
7	I am familiar with the inverted pyramid style of news articles and steps of writing a news article.					
8	I am able to write a fact-based news article using third person narration when assigned to.					
9	I have a better understanding of China's Internet celebrities and influencer economy.					
10	I have a better understanding of the impact of Internet celebrities and influencer economy on our daily life.					
11	I take pride in the fact that China's influencer economy is growing rapidly and some influencers help promote Chinese culture to the world.					
12	I would form a more critical view towards the Western coverage on Chinese KOLs, and if there are some misunderstandings, I would like to explain.					
13	I understand my role in the accomplishment of the project, and I have improved my teamwork skills by collaborating with my team members through peer interaction.					
14	After learning this chapter, I will tell stories about Chinese KOLs and influencer economy to international friends when I have the opportunity.					

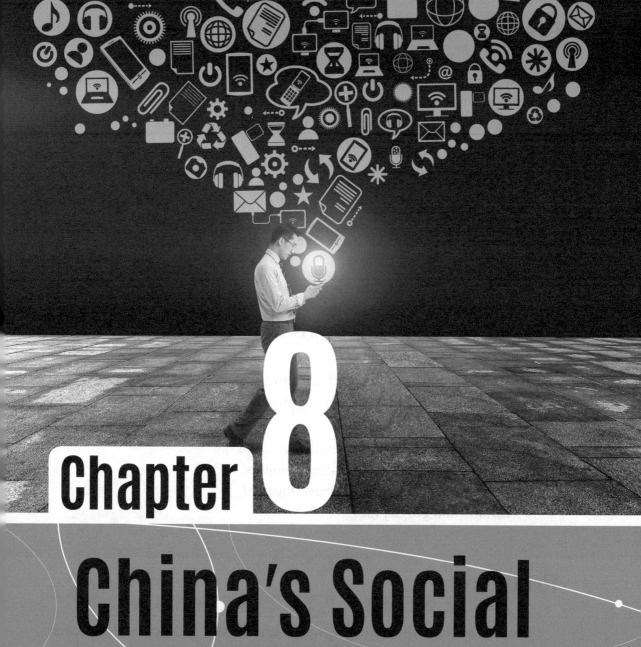

Chapter 8

China's Social Media

Pretest

How much do you know about social media in China? Can you match some key terms about social media with their proper explanations? You may go to our MOOC (5.2 Life in the Digital Age—Social Media) to learn more before taking this quiz.

1) an all-in-one messaging app

2) acting or dancing without words in sync with the music

3) content generated by users, such as the video you post on Douyin

4) a speed option you can choose to adjust your video to be posted online

5) an online activity through which knowledge is exchanged among all users

6) a technique through which all kinds of effect can be added to make your photo or video interesting

7) a technology company operating a range of content platforms that inform, educate, entertain and inspire people across languages, cultures and geographies

(　　) A. time lapse

(　　) B. filter

(　　) C. UGC

(　　) D. Bytedance

(　　) E. WeChat

(　　) F. miming

(　　) G. knowledge sharing

Pretask

You are currently working as an intern of MSRA (Microsoft Research Asia), and your team leader would like a briefing about major international media's portrayal of Chinese social media apps. You have received a piece of online article on TikTok, and your colleague advises you to write a summary of it.

1) To accomplish the task, I plan to take the following steps:

_____.

For the first step, I think _____

might be challenging.

For the second step, I think _____

might be challenging.

_____

_____

2) I expect to achieve the following goals after learning the unit:

_____

_____

Passage

How TikTok Is Rewriting the World

This article is adapted from John Herrman's article from The New York Times[1] *(March, 2019). The author sees through the popularity of TikTok and asserts that it is actually a game changer among all social media apps.*

refreshing /rɪˈfreʃɪŋ/
adj. pleasantly new or different; making you feel less tired or hot

sap /sæp/
v. to make sb./sth. weaker; to destroy sth. gradually

1   Hello, person who is, statistically speaking, a human adult aged approximately "millennial" to "boomer". The analytics suggest a high likelihood that you're aware there is an app named TikTok, and a similarly high likelihood that you're not totally sure what it's all about. Maybe you asked someone younger in your life, and they tried to explain and possibly failed. Or maybe you've heard that this new, extraordinarily popular video app is "a **refreshing** outlier in the social media universe" that's "genuinely fun to use". Maybe you even tried it, but bounce straight out, confused and **sapped**.

The Basic Human Explanation of TikTok

2   TikTok is an app for making and sharing short videos. The videos are tall, not square, but you

---

1 *The New York Times,* also known as the *Times,* is rated Left-Center biased based on word and story selection that moderately favors the Left, but highly factual and considered one of the most reliable sources for news information due to proper sourcing and well-respected journalists/editors.

navigate through videos by scrolling up and down, like a feed, not by tapping or swiping side to side.

3   Video creators have all sorts of tools at their disposal: filters as on Snapchat; the ability to search for sounds to score your video. Users are also strongly encouraged to engage with other users, through "response" videos or by means of "duets"—users can **duplicate** videos and add themselves alongside.

duplicate /ˈdjuːplɪkeɪt/
v. to make an exact copy of sth.

4   Hashtags play a surprisingly large role on TikTok. In more innocent times, Twitter hoped its users might **congregate** around hashtags in a never-ending series of productive pop-up mini-discourses. On TikTok, hashtags actually exist as a real, functional organizing principle: not for news, or even really anything trending anywhere else than TikTok, but for various "challenges", or jokes, or repeating formats, or other **discernible** blobs of activity.

congregate
/ˈkɒŋgrɪgeɪt/
v. to come together in a group

discernible /dɪˈsɜːnəbl/
adj. capable of being seen or noticed

5   TikTok is, however, a free-for-all. It's easy to make a video on TikTok, not just because of the tools it gives users, but because of extensive reasons and prompts it provides for you. You can select from an enormous range of sounds, from popular song clips to short moments from TV shows, YouTube videos or other TikToks. You can join a dare-like challenge, or participate in a dance meme, or make a joke. Or you can make fun of all of these things.

6   TikTok **assertively** answers anyone's what I should watch with a flood. In the same way, the app provides plenty of answers for the paralyzing what I should post. The result is an endless release of material that people, many very young, might be too self-conscious to post on Instagram, or that they never would have come up with in the first place without a nudge. It can be hard to watch. It can be charming. It can be very, very funny. It is frequently, in the

assertively /əˈsɜːtɪvli/
adv. in a strong and confident way, so that people take notice of what you think or want

engaging /ɪnˈɡeɪdʒɪŋ/
adj. interesting or pleasant in a way that attracts your attention

language widely applied outside the platform, from people on other platforms, extremely "cringe".

So That's What's on TikTok. What Is It?

7   TikTok can feel, to an American audience, a bit like a greatest hits compilation featuring only the most **engaging** elements and experiences of its predecessors. This is true, to a point. But TikTok—known as Douyin in China, where its parent company is based—must also be understood as one of the most popular of many short-video-sharing apps in that country.

8   Under the hood, TikTok is a fundamentally different app than those American users have used before. It may look and feel like its friend-feed-centric peers, and you can follow and be followed; of course there are hugely popular "stars", many cultivated by the company itself. There's messaging. Users can and do use it like any other social app. But the various aesthetic and functional similarities to Vine[2] or Snapchat or Instagram mask a core difference: TikTok is more machine than man. In this way, it's from the future—or at least a future. And it has some messages for us.

Instagram and Twitter Could Only Take Us So Far.

9   Twitter gained popularity as a tool for following people and being followed by other people and expanded from there. Twitter watched what its users did with its original concept and formalized the

---

2 Vine was an American social networking short-form video hosting service where users could share six- or seven-second long looping video clips. It was founded in June 2012 and was acquired by Twitter in October 2012.

conversational behaviors they invented. Only then, and after going public, did it start to become more assertive. It made more recommendations. It started reordering users' feeds based on what it thought they might want to see, or might have missed. **Opaque** machine intelligence **encroached** on the original system.

10 Something similar happened at Instagram, where algorithmic recommendation is now a very noticeable part of the experience, and on YouTube, where recommendations shuttle one around the platform in new and often let's say surprising ways. Some users might feel offended by these assertive new automatic features, which are clearly designed to increase interaction. One might reasonably worry that this trend serves the lowest demands of a **brutal** attention economy that is revealing tech companies as **cynical** time-mongers and turning us into mindless drones.

11 What's both crucial and easy to miss about TikTok is how it has stepped over the midpoint between the familiar self-directed feed and an experience based first on algorithmic observation and **inference**. The most obvious clue is right there when you open the app: The first thing you see isn't a feed of your friends, but a page called "For You". It's an algorithmic feed based on videos you've interacted with, or even just watched. It never runs out of material. It is not, unless you train it to be, full of people you know, or things you've **explicitly** told it you want to see. It's full of things that you seem to have demonstrated you want to watch, no matter what you actually say you want to watch.

12 It is constantly learning from you and, over time, builds a presumably complex but opaque model of what you tend to watch, and shows you

opaque /əʊˈpeɪk/
adj. (of speech or writing) difficult to understand; not clear

encroach /ɪnˈkrəʊtʃ/
v. (disapproving) to begin to affect or use up too much of sb.'s time, rights, personal life, etc.

brutal /ˈbruːtl/
adj. violent and cruel

cynical /ˈsɪnɪkl/
adj. not caring that sth. might hurt other people, if there is some advantage for you

inference /ˈɪnfərəns/
n. sth. that you can find out indirectly from what you already know

explicitly /ɪkˈsplɪsɪtli/
adv. clearly or directly, so that the meaning is easy to understand

viral /'vaɪrəl/
adj. like or caused by a virus

bar /bɑː(r)/
n. standard
grind /graɪnd/
v. to rub together, or to make hard objects rub together, often producing an unpleasant noise
simulate /'sɪmjuleɪt/
v. to create particular conditions that exist in real life using computers, models, etc., usually for study or training purposes
idly /'aɪdli/
adv. without any particular reason, purpose or effort
stiff /stɪf/
adj. difficult to bend or move
unmistakable /ˌʌnmɪ'steɪkəbl/
adj. that cannot be mistaken for sb./sth. else

more of that, or things like that, or things related to that, or, honestly, who knows, but it seems to work. TikTok starts making assumptions the second you've opened the app, before you've really given it anything to work with. Imagine an Instagram centered entirely around its "Explore" tab, or a Twitter built around, I guess, trending topics or **viral** tweets, with "following" bolted onto the side.

13 Imagine a version of Facebook that was able to fill your feed before you'd friended a single person. That's TikTok.

14 Its mode of creation is unusual, too. You can make stuff for your friends, or in response to your friends, sure. But users looking for something to post about are immediately recruited into group challenges, or hashtags, or shown popular songs. The **bar** is low. The stakes are low. Large audiences feel within reach, and smaller ones are easy to find, even if you're just messing around.

15 On most social networks the first step to show your content to a lot of people is **grinding** to build an audience, or having lots of friends, or being incredibly beautiful or wealthy or idle and willing to display that, or getting lucky or striking viral gold. TikTok instead encourages users to jump from audience to audience, trend to trend, creating something like **simulated** temporary friend groups, who get together to do friend-group things: to share an inside joke; to riff on a song; to talk **idly** and aimlessly about whatever is in front of you. Feedback is instant and frequently abundant; virality has a **stiff** tailwind. Stimulation is constant. There is an **unmistakable** sense that you're using something that's expanding in every direction. The pool of content is enormous. Most of it is meaningless. Some of it becomes popular, and some is great, and some

gets to be both. As *The Atlantic*'s[3] Taylor Lorenz put it, "Watching too many in a row can feel like you're about to have a brain freeze. They're incredibly addictive."

Why Do People Spend Hours on TikTok? It's the Machines.

16　All of this goes a long way to explain why, at least at first, TikTok can seem **disorienting**. "You're not actually sure why you're seeing what you're seeing," said Ankur Thakkar, the former editorial lead at Vine, TikTok's other most direct **forerunner**. On Vine, a new user might not have had much to watch, or felt much of a reason to create anything, but they understood their context: the list of people they followed, which was probably the thing letting them down.

17　"It's doing the thing that Twitter tried to solve, that everyone tried to solve," he said. "How do you get people to engage?" Apparently you just show them things, and let a powerful artificial intelligence take notes. You start sending daily notifications immediately. You tell them what to do. You fake it till you make it, algorithmically speaking.

18　American social platforms, each fighting their own desperate and often stock-price-related fights to increase user engagement, have been trending in TikTok's general direction for a while. It is possible, today, to receive highly personalized and effectively infinite content recommendations in YouTube without ever following a single account, because Google already watches what you do, and makes guesses about who you are. And while Facebook and Twitter don't talk

disorienting
/dɪsˈɔːrientɪŋ/
adj. causing loss of physical or intellectual bearings
forerunner /ˈfɔːrʌnə(r)/
n. a person or thing that came before and influenced sb./ sth. else that is similar

---

3　*The Atlantic* is an American lifestyle magazine and multi-platform publisher. It was founded in 1857 in Boston, Massachusetts.

about their products this way, we understand that sometimes—maybe a lot of the time—we use them just to fill time. They, in turn, want as much of our time as possible, and are quite obviously doing whatever they can to get it.

19   So maybe you'll sit TikTok out. But these things have a way of sneaking up behind you. Maybe you never joined Snapchat, but its rise worried Facebook so much that its prettier product, Instagram, was remade in its image, and copied concepts from Snapchat reached you there.

20   TikTok **does away with** many of the assumptions other social platforms have been built upon, and which they are in the process of discarding anyway. It questions the primacy of individual connections and friend networks. TikTok's real influence going forward may be that other social media platforms decide that our friends were simply holding us back. Or, at least, it was holding them back.

(1,761 words)

do away with
to terminate or take out

Theme-Related Words & Expressions

make and share short videos	制作和分享短视频
navigate through videos	浏览视频
scroll up and down	手指上下滚动
tap or swipe side to side	手指左右滑动
filter	滤镜
score a video	为视频配乐
duplicate videos	复制视频
hashtag	主题标签
pop-up discourse	突然弹出的对话
prompt	提示

popular song clips	流行歌曲片段
dance meme	舞蹈米姆
post	发布
nudge	拍一拍
short-video-sharing app	短视频分享应用
friend-feed-centric	以好友动态为中心的
follow and be followed	关注和被关注
hugely popular "stars"	大受欢迎的网红
cultivate "stars"	打造网红
messaging	消息发送
retweet	推特的转发功能
machine intelligence	机器智能
algorithmic recommendation	算法推荐
automatic feature	自动功能
increase interaction	增加互动
attention economy	注意力经济
self-directed feed	自导向信息源
"Explore" tab	"探索"标签
friend a person	加好友
group challenge	群组挑战
build an audience	建立一个受众群
simulated temporary friend groups	模拟临时朋友群组
riff on a song	即兴翻唱一首歌
instant feedback	即时反馈
list of people sb. follows	关注人列表
increase user engagement	提高用户参与度
content recommendations	内容推荐

Prepare/Probe

❶ Reading Comprehension

Answer the following questions according to the passage.

1) According to the author, TikTok is a free-for-all. What are the reasons?

   _____

   _____

2) How do you interpret the sentence "TikTok is more machine than man"?

   _____

   _____

3) Why does the author believe that "Instagram and Twitter could only take us so far"?

   _____

   _____

4) What makes TikTok mode of creation unusual?

   _____

   _____

5) What may be the real influence that TikTok will exert on other social media platforms? Why?

   _____

   _____

❷ Structure Building

Check your understanding of the overall structure of the passage by completing the following diagram.

Reasons for TikTok's Popularity	
It is easy to make videos on TikTok. (Paras. 2–6)	• It provides all sorts of 1) _____ for users such as filters and sounds to score your video.

Continued

	• Hashtags exist as a real organizing 2) _____ _____ for various "challenges", or jokes, or repeating formats, or other activities. • It provides extensive reasons and 3) _____ _____ for users, answering what you should watch and what you should 4) _____ .
Differences Between TikTok and Other Social Media Apps	
TikTok is different from other social apps. (Paras. 8–15)	**Other social apps (Twitter, YouTube, Instagram, etc.)** • A tool for 5) _____ and being followed by other people and expanded from there. • The first step to show your content is to build a(n) 6) _____ or having lots of friends. **TikTok** • It is more 7) _____ than man. • The "For You" page is an algorithmic feed based on videos you've 8) _____ . It keeps learning from you and builds a model of what you tend to watch, and 9) _____ videos that you might like.

Practice

❶ Vocabulary Practice

1. **Match the following theme-related words and expressions in Column A with their Chinese equivalents in Column B.**

Column A

1) filter

2) hashtag

3) score a video

Column B

A. 加好友

B. 为视频配乐

C. 算法推荐

4) algorithmic recommendation   D. 米姆 / 梗

5) follow accounts   E. 上下滚动

6) meme   F. 滤镜

7) friend a person   G. 复制

8) duplicate   H. 动态

9) scroll up and down   I. 加关注

10) feed   J. 主题标签

2. Group the words and expressions related to TikTok. You may find the words and expressions from Exercise 1 and the reading passage. Start with the examples given below.

Users	*millennial;* _____
Activities	*challenge;* _____
Tools & content	*filter;* _____
Technical terms	*algorithmic recommendation;* _____

3. Fill in the blanks with the words or phrases in the box. Change the form if necessary.

at one's disposal	likelihood	trial and error	prompt
trend	addictive	simulate	hashtag
engage with	in a row	scroll	

1) If you're a parent of a teen, there is a high _____ that your child is spending hours on TikTok.

2) To increase TikTok likes and followers, video creators have a range of tools and techniques _____.

3) Users can add _____ to their posts to categorize videos, increase visibility, and participate in challenges or jump on the latest meme bandwagon.

4) Due to this _____ nature of the type of content, it is very easy for people to keep watching too many random videos _____ on TikTok.

5) TikTok not only allows users to reach a wide audience, it also helps them meaningfully _____ other users.

6) The "For You" page is the page on TikTok with an endless feed; this means you can _____ up and down forever.

7) You can tap the "Share" button to share a video with friends. This will give _____ as to the methods for sharing: via WeChat, QQ, microblog, or direct message.

8) It doesn't matter if you are trying to _____ other popular content creators that went viral in the past and became famous on the platform.

9) I had tried many filters and techniques until finally, through _____, I came up with a way to duet with another video.

10) TikTok populates content based on user preferences, with videos featuring everything from top influencers and viral hashtags to _____ dances and challenges.

⬛ Sentence Practice

Study the sentence structure first, and then translate each of the given Chinese sentences into English by imitating the sentence structure.

1) The analytics <u>suggest a high likelihood that</u> you're aware there is an app named TikTok, <u>and a similarly high likelihood that</u> you're not totally sure what it's all about. (Para. 1)

翻译：中国与国际社会共同努力进行持续的碳减排行动，以应对气候变化带来的挑战。随着气候变暖，极端气候事件如野火、台风、洪水和干旱的发生可能性大为增加。

_____

_____

2) <u>It's easy to</u> make a video on TikTok, <u>not just because of</u> the tools it gives users, <u>but because of</u> extensive reasons and prompts it provides for you. (Para. 5)

翻译：中国企业在全球范围内的竞争力日益增强，不仅仅是出于成本原因，还出于质量和创新。

_____

_____

3) Some users <u>might feel offended by</u> these assertive new automatic features, <u>which are clearly designed to</u> increase interaction. (Para. 10)

翻译：企业的成功依赖于诚信和信任，或者至少是良好的沟通。

_____

_____

4) What's both crucial and easy to miss about TikTok is how it has stepped over the midpoint between the familiar self-directed feed and an experience based first on algorithmic observation and inference. (Para. 11)

翻译：中国的现代化不能是不切实际的，而应该加快努力发展一个由实体经济支撑的现代工业体系。

_____

5) All of this goes a long way to explain why, at least at first, TikTok can seem disorienting. (Para. 16)

翻译：在过去的十年里，我们在广泛的合作领域取得了长足的进步，并在新时代取得了合作的重大进展。

_____

_____

Ⅲ Discourse Practice

Complete the fragments with the suitable words or phrases in the box, and then sequence the fragments in the correct order. You may not use any of the words or phrases more than once.

| apart from that | in a nutshell | such as | as well as |
| second | third | first | due to |

A. _____ the short format, it's far easier to edit and upload content in TikTok than in other apps such as Instagram or Snapchat. Anyone with a smartphone can easily create and post content.

B. TikTok attracts users in so many ways. _____, it's convenient to use.

C. _____, TikTok is a popular, entertaining, and addictive app which allows users to watch, create, and share creative short videos.

D. TikTok is the world's leading short-video platform, which enables everyone to be a creator on a global stage. Since its launch, TikTok's popularity has been growing tremendously. It reportedly has amassed over 500 million monthly active users.

E. The algorithm measures how long they actually watch each video, _____ how many likes, comments, and shares it gets.

F. _____, TikTok enables everyone to be a creator, and encourages users to share their passion and creative expression through their videos. With varied interests and talents, users can create engaging content across themes _____ comedy, cooking, travel, DIY, dancing, and sports.

G. _____, TikTok uses advanced AI algorithms to learn user preferences and then provide customized video feeds to their users.

H. _____, the content they create is seemingly made for today's younger generation, who are most of the time glued on their smartphones and bored. It's appealing to their short attention span.

Sequence: _____

Produce

Write a Summary of "How TikTok Is Rewriting the World"

❶ Recap of the Previous Sessions

In Pretest, you've gained a basic understanding of social media in China. In Prepare/Probe, you've grasped the main idea and structure of the text. In Practice, you've familiarized yourself with the necessary language points, sentence patterns, and the key information needed for Produce. Now it's time to consider the production of a summary.

❷ Definition of a Summary

A summary is a brief restatement of essential thought of a longer composition. A good summary is concise, objective, complete (all key points) and original (in your own words). The purpose of a summary is to give the reader, in about 1/3 of the original length of an article or lecture, a clear, objective picture of the original article or lecture. Most importantly, the summary restates only the main points of an article or a lecture without giving examples or details, such as dates, numbers or statistics. Also do not include your own comments or evaluation in it.

Ⅲ Writing Techniques: Paraphrasing and Condensing

1. Definition of a paraphrase

A paraphrase is a restatement of a text, passage, or work giving the meaning in another form. When you paraphrase material from a source, you restate the information from an entire sentence or passage in your own words. When paraphrasing, it is important to keep the original meaning so that the facts remain intact, and you can change the sentence structure and use synonyms. If it is used in academic paper writing, the paraphrased words should also be referenced (because you are using someone else's ideas or information).

2. Steps of paraphrasing

Step 1: Identify the important information in the sentence and the relationship between points.

Step 2: Find out the linking devices and signal words within the article.

Step 3: Consider possible synonyms for the source vocabulary and change the part of speech (nouns to verbs, for instance).

For example:

Original: The price of a resort vacation typically includes meals, tips and equipment rentals, which makes your trip more cost-effective.

Paraphrase: All-inclusive resort vacations can make for an economical trip.

3. Definition of condensing

Condensing or condensation means the process of making a text shorter by taking out anything that is unnecessary. The process of condensation in creative writing is synonymous to precise writing.

4. Steps of condensing

Step 1: Go through the original text to grasp the general idea.

Step 2: Prepare a skeleton of basic structure by noting down the main points and key words.

Step 3: Exclude all the illustrations, elaborations and figurative expressions.

Step 4: Rewrite by joining the main points.

For example:

Original: The algorithm gives us whatever pleases us, and we, in turn, give the algorithm whatever pleases it. As the circle tightens, we become less and less able to separate algorithmic interests from our own.

Condensed: The interaction between algorithm and its users evolves a positive circulation, so users' interests become increasingly similar to that of the algorithm's.

Ⅳ Organization of a Summary

The structure of a summary includes three moves: M1 (Introduction), M2 (body) and M3 (conclusion).

M1: Organize your notes into an outline which includes main ideas and supporting points but no examples or details (dates, numbers, statistics).

Write an introduction that begins with the article's basic information (author, title, source and publication date) as well as a reporting verb (see the table below) to introduce the main idea. The article's main idea usually lasts one or two sentences, and the reporting verb is generally in present tense.

Argument/ Counter-argument	Neutral	Indication of results	Suggestion	Criticism
argue/argue against	state	show	suggest	criticize
assert/refute	note	demonstrate	recommend	
claim/rebut	report	illustrate		
contend	explain	indicate		
maintain	discuss	point out		

Continued

Argument/ Counter-argument	Neutral	Indication of results	Suggestion	Criticism
insist	illustrate	(studies/authors) prove		
posit	observe	(studies/authors) found		

M2: Mention the major aspects, factors or reasons that are discussed in the article.

Support your topic sentence with the necessary reasons or arguments raised by the author or lecturer but omit all references to details, such as dates or statistics.

Use transitional devices that reflect the organization and controlling idea of the original material, for example, cause-effect, comparison-contrast, classification, process, chronological order, persuasive argument, etc. In a longer summary, remind your reader that you are paraphrasing by using "reminder phrases". For example:

- The author goes on to say that...

- The article (author) further states that...

- (Author's last name) also states/maintains/argues that...

- (Author's last name) also believes/presents/suggests/tells us that...

- (Author's last name) supports...by using...

M3: Restate the article's or the lecturer's conclusion in one or two sentences. Be noted that the restatement is different from the phrasing of the introduction (M1). You may write like:

- The author concludes that...

- All in all, the article asserts that...

- Finally, it is concluded that...

- As a result, the author finishes the article with the idea that...

After you finish the steps above, you may reread the piece and make modifications in your second draft. In reviewing your first draft, you also need to check the use of tenses, personal pronouns, direct or indirect speeches, the length and the accurate delivery of the main ideas of your writing.

Post-Learning Evaluation

No.	Statements	Strongly agree	Agree	Not sure	Disagree	Strongly disagree
1	I have grasped the expressions related to the theme.					
2	I am familiar with the key words and phrases in the passage.					
3	I am familiar with the major points of the passage.					
4	I am familiar with the terms explained in the footnotes.					
5	I know how to use linking words in English writing.					
6	I know how to apply the skills of paraphrasing.					
7	I am familiar with the moves of summary writing.					
8	I am able to write a summary when assigned to.					
9	I understand my role in the accomplishment of the project, and I have improved my teamwork skills by collaborating with my team members.					
10	I will form a more critical view towards the Western coverage on China's social media, and if there are some misunderstandings, I would like to explain.					
11	I will share my view with international friends if they have any misunderstanding about China's social media.					

Continued

No.	Statements	Strongly agree	Agree	Not sure	Disagree	Strongly disagree
12	As a netizen, after learning this chapter, I have a better understanding of the importance of knowledge sharing in the era of social media.					
13	I take pride in TikTok's rapid advances in creating and sharing.					
14	After learning this chapter, I will tell the story of China's social media to international friends when I have the opportunity.					